To:

GRAHAM MY
BEST FRIEND -
HAPPY BIRTHDAY
— GIBO

NuSpeak™

Become a Powerful Speaker

State-of-the-Art Presentation Skills
by Geoffrey Lane

Requests for permission to reproduce any
part of this book should be mailed to:
NuMethod Education Inc.
PO Box 48181, Bentall Center, Vancouver, BC, V7X 1N8, Canada

Published by Berkana Books
PO Box 372, Bowen Island, BC, V0N 1G0, Canada

Cover design and artwork by
Parallel Strategies (Vancouver) Inc.
Layout by Carolyn Howse Graphic Design
Printed in Canada by Web ExPress International, Delta, BC

Canadian Cataloguing in Publication Data

Lane, Geoffrey, 1945-
NuSpeak: become a powerful speaker

Includes bibliographical references.
ISBN 1-894499-00-X

1. Public speaking. 1. Title

PN4121.L363 1999   808.5'1   C99-901236-3

Everything is out there waiting for you.
All you have to do is walk up and declare
yourself in. No need for permission.
You just need courage to say, "Include me."
Providing you have the energy to
pull it off, you can do what you like.
And the Universal Law, being impartial,
will be only too happy to deliver.
—Stuart Wilde

Dedication

This book is dedicated to those who, by their actions, strengthen the fabric of goodwill; the visionary volunteers at Leadership Vancouver; my friends and co-conspirators who have given time and encouragement to help in creating this vision—Alan, Cheryl, Helena, Sunshine, Judith, Georgia, Darlene, Graham, Gordon, Patricia, Deborah, David and Mary, Paul, Keith and Julie, Edward and Katherine, Bob and Franziska, David and Corinne; my wonderful family—Giovani, Lillie, Tom and Phyllis; our great children and their family, Mark and Mika, Kyle and Victoria; and my partner and inspiring friend, Loree, who daily demonstrates goodwill.

Acknowledgements

As I write this acknowledgement, many names, moments and faces come to mind. I would like to thank the following people for their invaluable contributions and inspiration:

- the facilitators, participants and friends from The Pursuit of Excellence series, particularly Dan Haygeman, Patricia Culver, Karen Grey, Jim Sorensen, Peggy Merlin, Randy and Judy Revell;

- the creative and questing team at Parallel Strategies, Catherine Worrall and Leigh Striegler, the graphic icons who assisted in the communication of the concept;

- Susan de Stein and Ian Edwards and the team at Verus, who helped me get the message out there;

- the team of NuSpeak facilitators and eternal students, Beth Gurszky, Terry Lineham, Dian Patterson, Suzette Watson, and Cathy Wilder, whose presence and seeking have taught me much;

- Olga Sheean, for her expertise in editing and communicating, without losing the intention or meaning—a gentle reminder to show up and be heard;

- Kendall Wilson and Nora Hunt-Haft, who have strengthened the purpose and direction of all those involved;

- Conrad Rademaker, whose faith and wisdom as a mentor through this process have been invaluable; and

- the many workshop participants whose individual contributions have benefited me greatly.

—Geoffrey Lane

Contents

Foreword

Throughout North America, there is a growing awareness of the vast human potential that remains largely untapped in most individuals. Performers, athletes and entrepreneurs are developing their inner strengths and abilities in order to achieve what they formerly believed to be impossible. One entrepreneur said that developing his presentation skills was the key element in helping him 'jump start' his career and 'leap frog' over colleagues who settled for a 'comfort zone' career.

Geoffrey Lane has created a powerful and comprehensive integration of the ancient art of oration with the modern techniques of authentic expression and values-based communication.

As a clinical psychologist, I have treated many people for the world's number-one phobia—the fear of public speaking. One of the best ways to overcome the fear of any new challenge is to have as complete a sense of mastery, control and understanding of the demands of that situation as possible. Geoffrey Lane has addressed that concern by writing the definitive book on presentation skills and personal effectiveness with any audience.

This is an ambitious book that offers authentic mentoring for both beginning and advanced practitioners of the speaking arts. It is a skillful blend of time-proven and original techniques, designed to produce powerful, confident speakers.

With a unique blend of humor, wisdom and practical applications, *NuSpeak* integrates the left-brain information (pacing, sequencing and common sense strategies) with right-brain teaching (stories, metaphors and wonderful visuals). This whole-brain approach to new learning is what distinguishes top educators and presenters from the rest of the pack.

As a professional and corporate speaker with over twenty years' experience, I only wish *NuSpeak* had been available to help me overcome my anxiety and discomfort in front of an audience when first starting out.

This is the most authoritative book yet written on the ancient art of oratory and public speaking. A must-read for all aspiring presenters.

Lee Pulos, PhD
Author of *The Power of Visualization*
and *Mentally Fit Forever*

Dr Lee Pulos is a master educator on peak performance, a leading authority on corporate and personal development, and a stress management counselor. As a sports psychologist, he has also worked with Olympic athletes and team Canada, and conducted coaching clinics throughout North America.

Introduction

Self-mastery: the art of showing up

If one really wishes to be a Master of an art,
technical knowledge is not enough.
One has to transcend technique
so that the art becomes artless art,
growing out of the unconscious.

Daisetz T. Suzuki

The challenge for the speaker is to become one
with the audience, sharing one reality.
This occurs when the speaker ceases to be
self-conscious as the one who is engaged in
speaking to the audience. Once it is realized
that both listener and speaker are one, there is
the possibility of some greater
form of communication.

Geoffrey Lane

Authentic Self-expression: the challenge of 'showing up'

I am encouraged when people show up and express themselves—when they take that step towards authentic self-expression. There is much fear in our world, and fear is often the reason we hide, or only reveal what we consider to be acceptable about ourselves.

I believe that the fear of revealing who we are is greatly misunderstood, and that that fear somehow equals the potential for the possibility of rejection by others. Yet most of us know instinctively when someone is hiding (i.e. not showing up) and consequently we do not trust them enough to reveal ourselves to them, or accept them for who they appear to be. In his book, *Seven Habits of Highly Successful People,* Stephen Covey describes the synergy and creativity that authentic self-expression brings:

"The more authentic you become, the more genuine in your expression, particularly regarding personal experiences and even self-doubts, the more people can relate to your expression and the safer it makes them feel to express themselves. That expression in turn feeds back on the other person's spirit, and genuine creative empathy takes place, producing new insights and learning, and a sense of excitement and adventure that keeps the process going."

It takes courage to risk the possible rejection that authenticity could bring. Yet being authentic (being our natural selves) is one of the greatest gifts we can offer other human beings and ourselves. When we are authentic, our quality of life is greatly enhanced, and there are many rewards. Our relationships improve and we experience less stress as a direct result of not hiding who we are. We develop deeper and longer-lasting friendships. Others in our community tend to trust us. The experience of the world seems more real. It seems to me that those who, by age or wisdom, live in the state of authenticity are respected, loved and admired.

I believe the need for personal communication is continually growing. The more we use technology—e-mail, voice mail, fax, and the Internet—to communicate with each other, the greater our need for face-to-face communication, and the more we crave the authenticity of personal contact. Nothing replaces the nuances of tone and pitch of a human voice or the facial and physical expressions of the communicator.

But because we are not using or developing these skills, we are losing our ability to 'show up.' Words are only part of the messages we send to each other; the emotion and intent are carried and amplified by the body language and sound of the human voice. Video conferencing adds another dimension, however nothing seems to replace the connection and understanding that come from the personal contact of a face-to-face meeting. When I show up in person and can be myself, I am heard in a very different way—a way that starts to build the relationship and deepen the understanding between listener and speaker. It creates an opportunity for a genuine exchange to take place.

Communicating in person is the most powerful form of human interaction. Show up and you will be heard and appreciated.

The Evolution of NuSpeak

The Romans of the first century considered the teaching of rhetoric and oratory to be very important, according to Quintillian, an influential Roman educator. In fact, they used Greek teachers and scholars to educate the existing and future leaders of Rome. However, the emphasis was on appearing knowledgeable, rather than on conveying facts or true wisdom. As Socrates said in Plato's *Gorgias*, "The Orator need have no knowledge of the truth about things: it is enough to have discovered a knack of convincing the ignorant that he knows more than the experts."

Although the organizational structure and form of oratory and rhetoric developed by the Ancient Greeks are still in use today, they have evolved considerably since those earlier times.

Philosophers and scientists have always been curious about why we behave and act the way we do, and today behavioral psychology, sociology, anthropology and physiology are now vast fields of study. The understanding of human behavior and motivation has been one of the major focuses of this century. The resulting accumulation of knowledge about how to influence, persuade and manipulate the human mind has been used to sell us ideas, goods and a way of life. This is achieved through the media, advertising, and propaganda, changing the way we see and experience the world. Not only have we become masters at using this information, we have also become masters at avoiding the strategies employed to sell and manipulate us.

The NuSpeak concept came about in response to requests for a new way of training in presentation and speaking skills. NuSpeak represents the way we need to present ourselves and communicate our message in this rapidly-changing and demanding world.

"How can I become a speaker/facilitator like you?" was a frequent question I was asked, challenging me to come up with an answer. In 1992, I started asking would-be speakers/facilitators what they really wanted, what kind of style they wanted to develop, what they liked about that style, and what they didn't like about speaking. Most people at first could only describe what they did not like, saying, for example:

- "I don't want to be lecturing people; I want to involve them;"
- "I don't want to sound or look like every other speaker from my club;"
- "I don't want to sound like an over-excited motivational speaker;"
- "I don't want to sound like my school teacher, my professor or my boss."

When most individuals start to develop their presentation skills, they tend to copy the behavior and style of those they consider to be good speakers. However, in the process, they leave behind that essential part that makes them unique—the natural or authentic self. As children, we are naturally ourselves, but as we grow up we model ourselves according to the behavior and strategies of our peers and parents, thus losing our uniqueness.

This important insight became apparent as a result of asking these questions. People wanted to be themselves, to let their real character show up when they were presenting, and they needed a new way of doing it! They wanted a method that enabled them to be relaxed, aware and skillful. I call this authentic self-expression. NuSpeak is a modern style of speaking that allows for this kind of expression. When you are being authentic, you do not need artifice or an 'ideal model' to live up to. This allows individuals to 'show up,' just as they would in normal conversation. By doing so, they are more effective and powerful in their communications.

Using my practical knowledge and experience, I created the workshop that is the basis for this book. It represents a synthesis of what I have learned while training and coaching individuals to express themselves authentically. Although it does not replace the experiential approach of a workshop, this book will increase your confidence and help you become a more effective communicator and skillful presenter.

It also has the potential to affect your life more positively than you may now imagine.

I believe we can all learn the skills involved in expressing ourselves, whether it is in front of two, two hundred or two thousand people. Our personal success depends on our ability to communicate our thoughts, feelings and ideas with clarity and passion! In my research, it became apparent to me that the same people demanding a new presentation model were also what I now call the NuAudience. This audience is educated, mobile, and somewhat cynical, with access to more information than any audience before them. They will check you and your information. Socrates' approach is no longer valid today. The demand for style has been replaced with a need for authentic and skillful self-expression.

We can't fake authenticity. Though we may sometimes feel the need to conform, in doing so, we destroy what we need most for authentic self-expression. Truth, substance, character and skills are the essential ingredients for success. I believe that acquiring these elements represents the first step towards achieving self-mastery and leadership. Values-based communication and the real you will have a powerful impact on your audience, inspiring them to act.

Show up and you will be heard.

The NuSpeak Concept

NuSpeak is organized around the following four elements, which represent the dynamics involved in a great presentation experience:

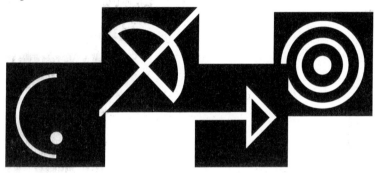

The ARCHER (which represents you, the presenter) provides the energy to shoot the arrow to the target. Learning how to manage, maintain and develop that energy is important and forms a major part of any presentation. The mind of the archer clearly focuses on the target, determining purpose, expected outcome, timing, speed, etc. This gives direction to the presentation so that the arrow can hit the target. The ground that the archer stands on represents his/her knowledge of the subject matter to be presented, as well as his/her skill at presenting.

The BOW represents the delivery system. What is the most effective medium through which to deliver the arrow—the message: overhead transparencies, slides, handouts, flip chart, audio-visuals, etc.

The ARROW represents the message or information to be delivered to the audience. The material must tell a story— just like a movie—whether it is sixty minutes, six minutes or sixty seconds long.

The TARGET represents the audience, which, for the presenter, is the most important element. The audience selects the type of event they wish to attend, whether for business, education or some other purpose. As a presenter, you need to know what motivates, interests and affects your audience. Read Chapter Four for the trends of the NuAudience.

This book can mark the beginning of your process of showing up and being heard. Practical experience will further enhance and strengthen your abilities as a communicator and presenter.

Your Personal Focus and Speaking Profile

Personal Focus

Developing a personal focus for using the material and exercises in this book will greatly enhance their value and significance for you. The following questions may help you achieve that focus:

1. How do you currently feel about presenting and speaking in public?
2. In your own words, what do you most want to achieve as a result of reading this book?
3. How will you feel when you have obtained this result?
4. What will you do with this new knowledge? (How will you put it to use?)
5. Why do you want this result?

Speaking Profile

Please take a few moments to reflect on the following speaking profiles and check off which type best describes you. By identifying your current level of experience and knowledge, you increase your opportunity for growth.

This describes me!   ☐ **Type A**
I am a white-knuckle speaker and avoid public speaking at all costs! I am terrified of groups watching me speak and want to learn how to master the fear, but don't know how.

This describes me!   ☐ **Type B**
I resist speaking and presenting in front of groups. I will do it, however I feel uncomfortable and anxious. I don't feel like an expert, but I would like to learn.

This describes me!   ☐ **Type C**
Nervous when it is a big group, okay with a smaller group. I would like to be able to handle all group sizes with less nervousness.

This describes me!   ☐ **Type D**
I give presentations as a part of my job. Most of the time, I feel I do a good job. I feel fairly competent, but I think I would enjoy it more if I had more confidence and training.

This describes me!   ☐ **Type E**
I used to make presentations on a regular basis, but am interested in upgrading my skills and adding a modern approach. I want to enhance my learning and enthusiasm.

This describes me!   ☐ **Type F**
I enjoy presenting and speaking, and look for every opportunity to improve my skills. The more I do, the better I feel. It is part of my work and I enjoy it.

① The Archer

"A man whose axe was missing suspected his neighbor's son of having stolen it. The boy walked like a thief, looked like a thief, and spoke like a thief. But the man found his axe while he was digging in the valley, and the next time he saw his neighbor's son, the boy walked, looked and spoke like any other child."

—Traditional German saying

The Archer (you, the presenter)

*You learn in life that the only person
you can really correct and change is yourself.*
—Katherine Hepburn

The role and functions of the Archer are composed of six distinct but interrelated parts:

1. **Focus.** The archer provides focus so that the arrow hits the target. This gives direction to the presentation, i.e. purpose, expected outcome, duration, speed, timing, composition of the audience, etc.

2. **Ability.** Your skill and experience at presenting also determine your ability to reach your audience.

3. **Preparation.** The archer builds the arrow (message) that flies true to the target, and chooses the most effective bow, given the environment. This represents your skill in preparing the material.

4. **Assessment.** In Olympic competition archery, the athletes take note of the wind direction, and the light conditions, and test their bows before firing their arrow. They adjust their finely tuned sights and bows to ensure the best possible result. Your ability to assess the physical and mental environment of the NuAudience helps in choosing the most effective tools to support your message.

5. **Energy management.** The archer provides the energy to shoot the arrow to the target. Physical and mental fitness

plays an important role for the successful presenter. This corresponds to your physical and mental state of being (which greatly affects the outcome of your presentation). Learning how to manage, maintain and develop that energy is important and forms a major part of any presentation. Developing a regular fitness regime will help with jet-lag, and mental fatigue, as well as providing the stamina required to deliver an energetic presentation.

6. **Foundation.** The ground that the archer stands on represents his/her knowledge of the subject matter to be presented. Ground is also the degree of comfort you feel in presenting. With sound knowledge and comfort, presenting becomes fun and exciting.

The 13 Deadly Sins of Presentations

> *There's a difference between interest and commitment. When you are interested in doing something, you do it only when it is convenient. When you are committed to something, you accept no excuses, only results.*
>
> —Raven

When leading my workshops, I ask participants what they dislike most about presenters, from the listeners' point of view. Over the last four years, the responses have been largely consistent, and include the following (italicized text represents my comments based on participants' observations and feedback from the NuAudience):

1. **Poor first impression. Not real. Faking it.**
   Not showing up. This represents a lack of energy or enthusiasm on the presenter's part.

2. **Starting or ending late.**
   This shows disrespect for the listeners' time and attention. It appears unprofessional and ill prepared.

3. **No objectives stated out loud to the audience.**
   They don't know where the presenter is going and, if he/she doesn't tell them, they will draw their own conclusions.

4. **Lack of conviction, no energy.**
   This is considered to be lack of interest on the presenter's part. Why would he/she talk about something he/she did not care about? The NuAudience won't care unless the speaker does.

5. **Dull, dry and boring.**
   Today's audience wants to be educated and entertained.

6. **Frozen in one spot.**
   When the presenter is frozen, so is the audience. In normal conversation, people move, gesticulate and display energy.

7. **Weak eye contact.**
   This makes the audience uneasy, making them wonder what is wrong and why the presenter is afraid to look them in the eye. This creates distrust and distance.

8. **No audience involvement.**
   The audience doesn't want to be ignored. They are the reason the presenter is there.

9. Poor facial expression.

   The audience wants the speaker to be natural. It is okay to smile or even frown, as long as you are being authentic.

10. No humor.

    This does not mean that the presenter should tell jokes, but it does mean that he/she should be natural and have a sense of humor about him/herself. It's good to take your presentation seriously, but not yourself.

11. Poor personal presentation.

    Presenters should dress to suit the occasion and the audience, paying attention to anything about their person that might distract the audience from hearing their message.

12. Poor visual aids.

    Presenters should have their material professionally prepared if it is a vital presentation. They can prepare their own if they are comfortable with any of the numerous presentation software programs.

13. Weak conclusion.

    Good presenters don't whimper away or seem apologetic for what they've said. They finish with some call to action, inspiring their audience to do something as a result of their presentation.

How to Show Up and Be Heard

While one person hesitates
because he feels inferior,
the other is busy
making mistakes
and becoming superior.

—Raven

Young children are naturally authentic and have no inhibitions about showing their excitement and enthusiasm. As adults, we have been socialized to the point that enthusiasm feels unnatural. Yet being enthusiastic is a powerful way of 'showing up.' Enthusiasm is often suppressed by presenters, as they wish to appear professional or cool, and certainly not overly excited. Most are afraid of looking like a 'motivational speaker.'

All energy is contagious, and this is particularly true of enthusiasm. Let your audience know that you're committed to your ideas and that you're excited about them. They'll not only see your enthusiasm, they will feel it and be moved or inspired in some way by your honest self-expression.

Enthusiasm is not the exclusive domain of a coach's pep talk or a hard-sell delivery. You may speak softly with heartfelt enthusiasm. You may be enthusiastically silent. You may passionately present your ideas in your own style.

If it's important enough to talk about, there's some room for enthusiasm. If you can't muster at least genuine conviction for the subject of your talk, perhaps someone else should give it.

Developing Energy

> *The depth of your conviction persuades people*
> *more than the height of your logic—more by*
> *your enthusiasm than any proof you can offer.*
>
> —Anonymous

We all have triggers that access certain states of mind. The state in which you drive your car, for example, is triggered by the simple act of turning the key in the ignition. Most of us, at some point, have driven somewhere while deep in thought, and arrived at our destination without being able to fully remember how we got there. I believe that this is because our subconscious accesses the state of consciousness associated with driving, automatically putting us into that mode of operation. My 'getting ready for work' state of consciousness includes taking the dog for a walk and then reading the morning paper. My wife insists that I am not even awake.

A series of simple affirmations (see following page), repeated enthusiastically, can act as a trigger to access the state we call enthusiasm. In order to anchor this state, these phrases must be stated loudly with plenty of physical action, and repeated many times each day for at least a month. If you can, use an area similar to that where you will be doing your presentation. Make sure you are not disturbing others, since they might find your behavior a little odd.

As you develop energy to help you 'show up,' one of the side effects is that you will feel less anxious when you are at the front of the room. It will also help your breathing and you will become accustomed to hearing your voice at a louder level. Whatever you do, have fun with this, and don't take it too seriously. It is meant to be slightly ridiculous in order to help you break free from any awkwardness you may have as a presenter. I have had people from all walks of life use this process. *It works!*

"When I access enthusiasm,

I *feel* enthusiastic.

When I *feel* enthusiastic,

I *am* enthusiastic."

As you make your way to the front of the room to give your presentation, repeat the phrase under your breath. When you get there, you will discover you have more energy and enthusiasm. It will help you 'show up,' have fun and be heard.

The Great Cultural Myth

*Nothing is so much to
be feared as fear.*
—Henry David Thoreau

According to comedian Jerry Seinfeld, "most people at a funeral would rather be in the coffin than giving the eulogy." We seem to have adopted the collective belief that presenting is a terrible experience, worse than death. A documented survey from the *Book of Lists* (Wallace and Wallechinsky, 1977) reflects this cultural myth in its list of the top ten human fears:

The top ten human fears:

1. Speaking before a group
2. Heights
3. Insects and bugs
4. Financial problems
5. Deep water
6. Sickness
7. **Death**
8. Flying
9. Loneliness
10. Dogs

The intense fear of public speaking can, unfortunately, become a self-fulfilling prophecy. Those who use their skills to dominate meetings and public events will continue to perpetuate the myth, all the while enjoying the admiration of those intimidated by their own fears.

Like any skill, the art of successful presentation can be learned and, once mastered, enjoyed as a truly fulfilling experience. It does not have to be a fearful death-defying event. Old-style training methods are aimed at helping you to tolerate the fear. NuSpeak is designed to increase your understanding of the process and eliminate the fear. I remember hearing the story of a scientist who put a frog in a container of cool water, and then very slowly raised the temperature, a fraction of a degree at a time. The frog did not move and eventually boiled to death! Getting used to the fear is like boiling to death your natural and authentic self-expression. Don't become someone else's ideal definition of a good presenter. Define it yourself. The audience of today can smell phoniness a mile away. Faking it till you make it will not work.

Making a Paradigm Shift

> *Those who risk nothing become enslaved*
> *and forfeit their freedom. They simply cannot*
> *experience the full range of life. To change,*
> *grow, and love is the greatest risk of all,*
> *bringing the greatest of rewards.*
> *Only those who risk are truly free.*
>
> —Geoffrey Lane

**Question: What do you think
comes first: belief or experience?
Answer: I'll give you a clue:
what do you *believe* comes first?"**

Each of us grows up believing that our cultural point of view is the best or right point of view. This ethnocentricity (whereby one regards one's own culture as the most important) develops naturally as we unconsciously absorb many of the views of our primary caregivers early in life. When we travel and mix with other nationalities, we have the opportunity to realize that each culture has its own point of view, and believes it to be the right one. Often we invalidate new experiences by comparing them with our own cultural point of view, rather than seeking to understand them with an open mind.

Our assumptions and beliefs determine our attitudes, before we are even aware of having chosen them. This unconscious process acts like a stained-glass window between us and the world, coloring our outlook and distorting what we see. Our gender, parents, extended family, friends, education, age, the society we live in and our social status all color our view of the world.

I create my point of view of the world and myself in the following way:

> Because I think what I think (my beliefs),
> I do what I do (actions based on beliefs).
>
> Because I do what I do, I get what I get—i.e.
> results based on actions that are based on my beliefs.

My beliefs filter my view of the world. I determine them myself and am responsible for the actions I take as a result, although I may not always be aware of why I act a particular way.

Our point of view (paradigm of reality) defines our limits and our capabilities, setting the parameters for our success and happiness. The fact that our beliefs are mostly invisible can result in an interesting paradox. Until we realize that we are constantly viewing the world through our beliefs, and that our view is constantly filtered by what we have determined those beliefs to be, it is easy for us to think that we are seeing life as it really is.

The results that I obtain in my life are the true measure of my point of view of the world and of myself. Therefore, if I believe that I can't speak publicly, I will most likely prove myself right. I will find evidence to support my point of view. I will find others who also subscribe to this point of view. I will avoid the act of public speaking and, even if I force myself to do it, I will not enjoy it. I will admire those who do speak publicly, thinking, "rather them than me." In so doing, I will support and magnify the great cultural myth that there is nothing more terrifying than speaking before a group.

Most of the fear of showing up and speaking is based on false expectations appearing real.

F **false**

E **expectations**

A **appearing**

R **real**

False expectations occur because most of us believe the cultural myth that we should fear speaking in public. We are afraid of what I call 'social death'—being embarrassed and not liked or accepted by others. In reality, the audience does not react to us this way. Most of them admire anyone who gets up. This is because they too believe 'The Myth.' They judge you favorably because you have the courage to stand up and speak. I call this 'The Halo Effect' (see the Target section).

Our expectations can work equally well in our favor. And a strong positive belief can even be good medicine, as the following story illustrates. In the mid-1950s, a man by the name of Wright was dying of cancer of the lymph nodes when he learned that a new, highly promising cancer drug, Krebiozen, would soon be available for trial. He begged his doctors to test it on him even though his high fever and the large tumors in his neck meant he was too sick to qualify for the experiment. Wright insisted and the doctors gave in. He received his first dose of Krebiozen on a Friday and, by Monday, he was walking around the ward, chatting with the nurses. His tumors had melted.

But then things took a nasty turn. The drug trial proved to be a flop. Wright followed the bad publicity about Krebiozen in the newspapers and suffered a relapse. But then his doctor, Philip West, had an idea. He told Wright that the drug had not been strong enough and that a new double-strength Krebiozen was on its way. Then Dr West injected Wright with nothing more than sterile water. Wright rebounded again and stayed that way until the American Medical Association made a formal announcement that Krebiozen was a worthless drug for treating cancer. A short while after the announcement, Wright died.[1]

Research into the placebo effect (a positive outcome based on a positive expectation) also revealed the 'nocebo effect' (a negative outcome based on a negative expectation). (Dr Herbert Benson explores this phenomenon thoroughly in his book, *Timeless Healing*.) It follows, then, that if I expect to have a good time, generally I do, and the reverse is also true. What I believe, I tend to create.

Appearances can be deceptive. We often see what we want to see, or are afraid we will see, depending on our perspective. Our window on the world is colored by our point of view (beliefs).

Reality is often different from our expectations. If our belief is false to begin with, then our expectations will also be false and will never match reality. It is normal to experience the rush of adrenaline as you get up to speak. Most of us only experience this when the fight or flight reflex is triggered, such as when we are threatened or faced with personal danger (e.g. someone suddenly pulling in front of you on a busy highway). This adrenaline coursing in our veins can cause extra anxiety because it feels uncomfortable and is normally associated with personal danger.

The Conscious and the Unconscious

*Take care to get what you like
or you will be forced to like what you get.*
—George Bernard Shaw

Many people claim that most forms of reactive behaviors are unconscious, yet, to me, it's quite evident that we are not unconscious of some of the behaviors that we don't like about ourselves. On the contrary; we are often all too conscious of their effect in our lives.

It might therefore be more accurate to say that these patterns of behavior are outside of our current consciousness or awareness. There is considerable evidence to indicate that the phenomenon we call 'consciousness' is the result of what we are currently focused upon; it is our awareness of things, and it's through this focus that we screen and translate the effects into reality. Based on that level of awareness, we make sense of reality.

For example, in order for you to understand or appreciate the words that I'm using right now, your mind has to translate the words somewhere outside of your current consciousness and make the meaning of those words known to you other than consciously.

The unconscious handles many functions for us—things that we are not focused on and can do automatically. For example, breathing isn't something we normally consciously focus on unless we lack oxygen. Many things float up from our unconscious when it decides that something requires our urgent attention. I have often been leading a workshop, highly focused on the participants, and unaware of any bodily discomfort or needs. Then, during the break, I suddenly become aware of how sore my feet are and then my focus immediately shifts to my feet. My unconscious had handled the discomfort until the break, enabling me to focus on the workshop when I needed to.

This wonderful ability allows us to focus and create. However the unconscious does have a primary function: it is designed to keep us safe and to ensure the survival of the species. In moments of extreme danger, individuals often perform heroic physical feats, and parents have sacrificed themselves in order to save their children.

The unconscious will also attempt to assist you in creating what you want, motivating you towards pleasure and away from pain. Imagine, then, what would happen if you believed that speaking before a group was painful and somehow represented social death! Your unconscious would probably attempt to stop you from ever speaking, creating tension and anxiety in your body. If you did stop yourself from speaking, you would experience temporary relief from the anxiety. Only later would you perhaps experience anxiety because you did not speak up.

I believe that most of us don't 'show up' because of the power of our fears and the power of our unconscious. Many people attempt to get used to the anxiety of presenting, but I suggest that this is usually not a healthy solution. I believe that, by changing your point of view, increasing your knowledge and developing your skill set, you can make a paradigm shift in this area. Knowledge and understanding are fear killers, enabling you to let go of 'The Myth.' I have witnessed this often in workshops. When the shift occurs, presentations suddenly become exhilarating and fun.

Creating a New Paradigm

> *A happy person is not a person in a certain set*
> *of circumstances, but rather a person with a*
> *certain set of attitudes.*
>
> —Raven

It is possible to change your belief about public speaking, and I see it happen regularly. The greatest challenge seems to be that of letting go of past beliefs concerning public speaking.

We are often unaware of the fact that many of our choices and actions are determined by past beliefs, myths and experiences. But unless we are conscious of what drives or hinders us in a given area of our lives, there is little we can do about it. This lack of awareness makes it difficult for us to cast off the anchor of the past belief. Fortunately, however, the same is true with regard to our attachment to all the moments of success and achievement that we have experienced.

Most of you have an ideal picture of the kind of presenter you would like to be. But if you compare this with your actual situation, bearing in mind the myth that public speaking is the number-one fear among North Americans, you may start to feel tense and anxious. So how do you motivate yourself to take the next step? I believe the answer is to shift your point of view about past beliefs. Your past experiences have brought you to where you are today, and the past can also serve you in creating a powerful, positive future.

So how do we transform the past into a useful resource for creating what we want? In school, I remember my history teacher saying, "Unless we learn from the past, we are doomed to repeat it." When I turn my personal 'past' into 'history,' I am able to use my experience and knowledge without attachment.

This is not necessarily a matter of letting go. It is about creating a new paradigm of reality based on what is currently happening.

Perception is key to this process. To use an analogy, consider the similarities between a piece of coal and a one-carat diamond. They are both made of carbon, but one has remained in its crude form, whereas the other has been formed under pressure and then polished to give it form and brilliance. Although transformed, the diamond is still essentially carbon.

It takes some work and courage to bring yourself into current reality concerning presentations. It requires an objective look at your current knowledge about the subject, and the experience and resources you bring to the learning cycle. It also means turning your past thoughts and beliefs about presentation skills into history. It means letting go of the unattainable 'ideal' and being you.

Imagine for a moment that I were to give you two pails full of water—one marked 'The Past,' and the other marked 'Old Strategies that Work.' If you are holding onto these two pails and you see before you a pail of water marked 'Future,' what will you need to do in order to move forward? You will have to let go of one of the pails you are carrying—either the 'Past,' or 'Old Strategies that Work'—in order to access your Future. You may find it difficult, or even impossible, to let go of your past and the strategies that have worked for you up to now. I suggest that the solution is to distill the contents of both pails down to the rare essences of your successes and experiences. You would then have the essential ingredients with which to create your future, and the ability to move forward unburdened.

Getting to Current Reality

> *I have realized that the past and
> future are really illusions, in that they
> exist only in the present, which is
> what there is and all that there is.*
>
> —Alan Watts

The following exercise is designed to provide you with a vehicle for looking at your past and bringing yourself up to date. This information gathering provides the material for the next step. It will help you bring yourself into current reality. When you have completed this exercise, notice any patterns or strategies you have used to accomplish these results.

Exercise 1
Write out a list of:
- All your accomplishments, big and small, i.e. obtaining your driver's license, university degree, managerial position, becoming a parent, volunteering, etc.
- All the different lessons you have learned over your lifetime: the good, the bad, the ugly—whatever you have learned as a result of your experience.
- The goals you have reached, i.e. buying a home, gaining a promotion, completing a project in the garden, going on a foreign vacation, etc.

Include all areas of your life:
- Relationships
- Family
- Academic achievement
- Work achievement

- Spiritual growth and philosophy
- Play

Examine your life from birth to the present day, using five-year increments, until you reach today's date.

Developing Creative Tension

> *If you advance confidently in the direction of*
> *your dreams and endeavor to live the life you*
> *have imagined, you will meet with a success*
> *unexpected in common hours.*
> —Henry David Thoreau

Converting the past into history frees up the energy it takes to hold onto 'the way it was.' This also gives you greater objectivity with which to develop a clear picture of what you now want, based on current reality.

This inevitably creates tension between where you are now (current reality) and the results you wish to obtain in your future reality. In his book, *The Fifth Discipline Fieldbook,* Peter Senge refers to this as 'Creative Tension.'

Using the material gathered during Exercise 1, use the following process to help you to develop your own 'creative tension.'

Step 1. Examine the information from a different point of view, using the following questions as a guide. Who created these results? Who learned the skills in order to create these results? If you can create these results, can you create new results using the same or new strategies?

Notice your answers. The important thing to remember here is that you learned all of the strategies that got you to where you are today. You learned them, and if you can learn one thing, you can learn many. Even though you had the influence and guidance of others, it is you who created the results in your life. Like it or not, you are that person.

Step 2. Now describe yourself based on the information you have today. Bring yourself forward to current reality. Describe the presenter that you are today, in current terms, using "I am..." statements.

Step 3. Ever found yourself wondering why you did something? I believe that unless you consciously create something, your unconscious will create it for you, based on your past wants and needs. To avoid creating what you don't want, you therefore need to develop a clear vision and a series of measurable and identifiable goals. This will help determine what will manifest in your life.

Identify the kind of presenter you want to be (future reality), based on your known abilities (current reality), acknowledging that change can and does happen regularly. Here are some questions you might ask yourself:

- What style of speaker have I decided to be?
- What key phrase describes me?
- What three unique qualities do I possess as a speaker?
- Who is my target audience?
- What are my best assets as a speaker?

With the answers, build a clear picture of the speaker/presenter you want to become. Consciously create your vision based on who you are.

Many participants in my workshops have found that this process can be constructively applied to all areas of their life. Start with your presentation and communication skills first. Notice what you learn, and learn how to use the process for yourself. My wife and I use this process every year on New Year's Eve. We take some time to assess where we have been and then acknowledge where we are (current reality). Then we re-commit to our personal and joint visions. I personally go through a re-assessment process before each workshop or speaking event, as it helps me focus and 'show up.'

Staying Grounded

> *To thine own self be true.*
> *And it must follow, as the night the day,*
> *thou canst not then be false to any man.*
> —William Shakespeare

The following process is powerful when you have chosen to commit to your personal vision. The challenge is maintaining the creative tension necessary to achieve your vision in the midst of daily stresses and demands. The following questions will help you ground yourself in current reality, and re-focus on your vision.

Challenge yourself to ask these questions when you are in need of re-focusing, such as in moments of stress or confusion. This will develop the habit of staying in current reality. Start by asking, "What do I want?" then proceed with the following four-step exercise process.

Step 1: Ask yourself, "What is happening right now? What am I doing right now? What am I feeling right now? What am I thinking right now?"

Step 2: Ask yourself, "What do I want right now?" In other words, ask yourself what you are trying to achieve in this moment. Asking yourself this question usually helps ground the energy and change the course of action, without you having to make a very deliberate decision to change.

Step 3: Ask yourself, "What am I doing to prevent myself from getting what I want?" At this point, make a choice (based on your personal vision). Say to yourself, "I choose..." and fill in the blank. With practice, you will find yourself doing this automatically and easily, regrounding in your course of action as early as the first question.

Step 4: Ask yourself, "What is it that I want to create now?" This will bring your focus back to the vision you are creating.

What's Unique about YOU?

> *The greatest waste of our natural resources is the*
> *number of people who never achieve their*
> *potential. Get out of that slow lane; shift into*
> *that fast lane. If you think you can't, you won't.*
> *If you think you can, there's a good chance you*
> *will. Even making the effort will make you feel*
> *like a new person. Reputations are made by*
> *searching for things that can't be done, and*
> *doing them.*

—a message from United Technologies Corporation, Hanford, CT, published in the *Wall Street Journal*.

The following exercise will help you to see and acknowledge your individual gifts and strengths.

Exercise 2

Step 1: Write down what you believe is unique about you.

Step 2: Ask eight friends to communicate what they think is unique about you. Add their comments to your own evaluation. Communicate in such a way that you do not influence their view of you. Be careful that you do not edit their comments based on your own preconceived ideas. Trust them to respond truthfully.

Step 3: Compare your own assessment with the feedback from those you approached for their input. Notice any similarity and disparity. Most of us lack perspective about ourselves, and we are our own harshest critic. This exercise is therefore helpful in providing you with a different perspective of yourself. Make sure you accept the compliments that your friends and peers send your way, rather than canceling them out by thinking, "If only you knew me."

This information is useful in several ways. It gives you an idea of your natural style of communication, and provides the basis for developing and strengthening your own presentation style. The feedback from this exercise will also help you see where you have been 'showing up' in your life—as well as where you have failed to show up and why.

Discovering your Natural Style

If you are master of yourself, everywhere,
then all that you do proves true.

—Zen saying

The clues to your natural style may be found in the answers provided by your peers and friends in Exercise 2. This gives you an indication of how you communicate in the world. The following process will further assist you.

Based on the feedback from your friends, and using the following guidelines, visualize yourself giving a highly successful presentation:

- Observe yourself walking out in front of your audience, striding with natural purpose and pride.
- Observe yourself using a conversational style, as if telling a story to a close friend.

- Observe your natural gestures begin to surface, as they do when talking with friends.
- Observe yourself smiling, using your natural facial expressions for added emphasis.
- Observe yourself standing naturally, allowing your arms to rest at your sides.
- Observe yourself making natural eye contact with each member of your audience, and holding that contact for at least three-to-six seconds.
- Observe yourself using natural story-telling techniques, creating strong images and using your voice as an instrument.
- Observe yourself using natural pitches and tempos to keep your listeners involved.
- Observe yourself tap into your natural vocal power.

Based on how you saw yourself presenting, identify and write down the elements of your natural style. This provides you with your own personal 'benchmark,' which helps you show up naturally, rather than unconsciously falling into the trap of 'acting' like someone you may admire, or changing your natural style to please someone else. Review yourself periodically. As you develop, you will change and more of 'you' will show up.

Are Two Brains Better than One?

Whenever we communicate with each other
correctly, there is an exchange of energy.
—Reshad Field, *Steps to Freedom*

Do you: Like to be systematic and structured? Like to work with your door closed? Create order and send memos? Call yourself conservative? Have a neat and tidy office? Prefer logic, rather than emotion?

If so, you are probably left-brain dominant.

Do you: Like to discuss things and talk out your ideas? Like to work with your door open? Have personal things in your office? Like to be demonstrative and relate to others?

If so, you are probably right-brain dominant.

Dr R. Sepeari received the Nobel Peace Prize for discovering that we all have two brains, a right and left, joined together by the corpus callosum—rather like the coaxial cable that connects the TV to the cable company (only much faster and more reliable). The two brains work together, but handle different functions. You are not exclusively right- or left-brained, but you will tend to rely on one more than the other.

As a left-brain-dominant individual, you will tend to be conservative, systematic, organized, introverted and good at research. You are very good at writing and organizing materials, and poor at delivering a presentation. You need to focus on the actual delivery or performance of the presentation; as a rule, you tend to over-prepare, and need to remember that your audience wants only the pertinent facts. Spend most of your time rehearsing and find a right-brain-dominant friend to listen to your presentation before you give it.

As a right-brain-dominant individual, you tend to be impulsive, creative, humorous, emotive and extroverted. You are very good at presenting (performing), but not very good at writing or organizing material. You need to focus on organizing in a coherent manner that will make sense to your audience. Remember to write your last sentence first, as it will act as a focus point. Find a left-brain-dominant friend to read your material before you present it, then learn it, and stay on topic and time.

For both left- and right-brain-dominant individuals, the key to better communication and presentations is to understand both approaches, and to recognize how each will tend to see the world, and communicate what they see. In order to have your message heard effectively, it is essential to learn about and appreciate both communication styles, since your audience will be made up of both.

If you feel comfortable in both the logical and emotive worlds, you are a rare and unique individual. Most of us need to work hard in order to understand the style opposite to our own—whether it be the logical, orderly mind versus the impulsive and creative mind, or the impulsive and creative mind versus the mind of logic and order.

Cerebral Hemisphere Function: styles of learning and thinking

Left Brain	Right Brain
Recognizes/remembers names	Recognizes/remembers faces
Responds to verbal instructions	Responds to visual and kinesthetic instructions
Uses systematic and controlled thinking	Is playful and loose-thinking
Is inhibited emotionally	Responds with emotion/feeling
Is dependent upon words for meaning	Interprets body language easily
Produces logical ideas/thoughts	Produces humorous ideas/thoughts
Is serious and systematic in solving problems	Playful in solving problems, uses humor, experiments
Likes to have a definite plan	Likes to improvise
Is not psychic	Is highly psychic
Makes little use of metaphors and analogies	Makes frequent use of metaphors and analogies
Is logical in solving problems	Is intuitive in solving problems
Uses language in remembering	Uses images in remembering

—From *Your Style of Learning and Thinking*, by E. Paul Torrance.

It is my observation that you are not 'stuck' in any one style. However, most people have a preferred (more comfortable) style that is not always effective in presentations. It seems that those who are not 'natural speakers' often become the most effective, perhaps because they possess the dedication and focus to study and apply what they learn. With time, practice and dedication, however, anyone can become an effective presenter.

The Olympic Champions' Strategy

The farmer channels water to his land.
The fletcher whittles his arrows.
The carpenter turns his wood.
And the wise man directs his mind.

—The Buddha

When the last winter Olympics where being televised from Nagano, Japan, there was a delay due to heavy snowfall. In the gate, waiting to ski the Giant Slalom, stood an athlete, eyes closed. He was swaying back and forth, and the sports commentator pointed out that he was probably mentally rehearsing his run.

Many Olympic athletes give themselves one workout that does not involve breaking out in a sweat. It is one in which they 'see' themselves successfully competing and winning their event. Some do it with guided visualization, listening to a tape, whereas others just see themselves in their mind's eye and add some physical movements. Both approaches are an effective means of improving your results, according to Dr Lee Pulos, a psychologist who has coached Olympic athletes. In his tape series, called *The Power of Visualization*, Dr Pulos outlines this process in detail: see yourself doing it, see yourself in action, and experience the positive result.

Many people naturally use visualization without being aware that they are doing so. Often, the night before an important presentation event, they become tense as they imagine themselves making a complete fool of themselves! This, in turn, increases their anxiety and reinforces the myth and fear of public speaking. By visualizing themselves failing, they have set up the mechanism for a self-fulfilling prophecy to unfold.

Instead, why not use this process to your advantage. See yourself arriving. Notice how good you look. Feel what you are wearing. See yourself smiling with anticipation. Notice the audience smiling with you. Feel how calm and aware you are. Hear yourself making the presentation. Notice how firm and clear your voice is. Experience yourself remembering everything. Hear yourself answering questions confidently and easily. See the smiling faces of the audience admiring you. Hear the applause when you have finished. Feel the praise for a job well done.

At the very least, this workout will help you relax and increase the possibility of a positive result. It may also be helpful to record these cues onto an audiotape. Make sure you give yourself some time between each one so that you can see, feel and hear the experience that you are seeking. One person I coached recorded his entire speech in the middle of the guided instructions and found that it worked very well for him.

A word of caution: if you do this in bed, with your eyes closed (as I do), make sure you have set your alarm for the morning. You just might fall asleep, and get a good night's rest.

---

1. "Psychological Variables in Human Cancer," *Journal of Projective Techniques and Personality Assessment,* volume 21 (1957).

② **The Bow**

Aim for success, not for perfection. Never give up your right to be wrong, because you will lose the ability to learn new things and to move forward with your life. Remember that fear always lurks behind perfectionism...
Confronting your fears and allowing yourself the right to be human can, paradoxically, make you a far happier and more productive person.

—Dr David M. Burns

The Bow

> *Music is your own experience, your thoughts,*
> *your wisdom. If you don't live it, it won't come*
> *out of your horn.*
> —Charlie Parker

The Bow represents the various tools the presenter might use to increase the effectiveness of his/her presentation.

To ensure success, the Archer needs to identify the most effective tool for enhancing his or her message, bearing in mind the audience and the environment. Here are some of the tools that can be used:

1. Handouts/prepared flip charts
2. Flip chart
3. Transparencies
4. Slides
5. Models
6. LCD (liquid crystal display) high-intensity projectors
7. Computer-generated slide shows
8. Video or digital clips
9. Audio clips
10. Natural voice
11. Lavaliere microphone
12. Wireless microphone connected to a public address system or through soundboard for modulation of tone and pitch
13. Natural look or make-up
14. Dressing so as to fit in and belong
15. Dressing for dramatic effect in order to separate yourself from the audience

Most presentations today have audiences of ten-to-twenty-five people, so you will need to choose your audio-visual support tools according to your environment.

The Greatest Audio-visual: You

When one is willing and eager, the gods join in.
—Aeschylus

Non-verbal communication

Given that most business audiences and meetings number less than 25, you can usually be seen very clearly, regardless of all the props you might use. Remember that you are the most important audio-visual you have!

At the 1999 Academy Awards ceremony, Italian actor/director Roberto Benigni, the winner of two Oscars, demonstrated what an effect enthusiasm and joy can have on an audience. In accepting his first award for Best Foreign Film, he was so natural and real that, even with his limited use of English, the jaded Hollywood audience responded with loud and long applause. When he was awarded a second Oscar for Best Actor, Roberto leapt to his feet and started to walk on the backs of the theatre chairs. By the time he got to the stage to accept his Oscar, much of the audience were on their feet. When he finished his acceptance speech, they gave him a standing ovation!

Even with limited English skills, Roberto's message was heard loud and clear.

Gwyneth Paltrow was also genuine in accepting her Oscar. The references to her family and grandparents struck a strong chord in the hearts of the audience. She suddenly became 'real' to many who had experienced her only as an actress. As Will

Rogers reminds us, "That which is most personal is also most general," and yet this is often what we self-censure in our expression. Gwyneth Paltrow, in her genuine and emotive recognition of her family, not only connected with herself and her fans, but also created many new ones as a result of her authentic self-expression.

Two years before, Cuba Gooding Jr also brought the house down with his joyful and enthusiastic reaction to winning an Oscar as Best Actor in the movie *Jerry McQuire.*

All of these winners allowed themselves to 'show up' enthusiastically and received standing ovations, as a result. They were not acting; they were being themselves. In spite of the pressure of the event, they provided a rare moment of authentic self-expression.

The Impact of your Presentation

The breakdown of the various factors that determine the overall impact of your presentation reveals the following significant percentages:

7% Words

38% Voice

55% Body Language

Actions speak louder than words

Source: Professor Albert Mahrabian, University of California, LA.

Visual Aids Preparation

> *If you want something you have never had,*
> *you must be willing to do*
> *something you have never done.*
> —P. Aaron

Arrange your visual aids to follow your presentation script, as this helps you stay on track and is easier for the audience to follow. Use the visuals as the prompter for your presentation. The following practical tips will help you remain calm, focused and professional:

- Use the KISS principle: Keep It Simple and Superb.

- Use one idea and an average of three lines of text per slide.

- Rehearse each step.

- Illustrate your key points with pictures, graphs and charts. There are many sources of visual material: newspapers, magazines, photographs and video clips. Use all available modern resources, such as clip-art, cartoons and software programs specializing in presentations.

- Be bold, be brilliant, be big!

- Prepare the flip chart. If you are going to be using a flip chart, you can make things easier by using an overhead projector to project any graphs or images onto the flip chart. Trace the images lightly with a pencil in advance. You can then draw those images later in your presentation.

- Practice drawing on the flip chart using different colors and pen thickness. Get yourself a light-blue-squared chart and practice writing in block letters, which are easier to read than normal handwriting.

- Before you start, remember to check your slides. Someone could have changed the order. Once you have started, it is too late to rearrange them.

- Find the 'on' switch. Practice using the overhead projector, or the liquid crystal display projector and the computer that runs it.

- Take a class on the use of the computer software program that you and your company use. Learn the techniques and commands available, however do not try to use every one of them in the same presentation.

- Be ready when your support systems do not work! You are the presenter and the audio-visual aids only support your energy and focus.

Using Visual Aids

> *As a man is, so he sees.*
> —William Blake

Remember the 10% rule: less is more effective. Use a few well-conceived visuals that are memorable, rather than many ordinary, boring charts or slides. Keep the number of words per visual to a minimum. Use headlines only; better still, use short phrases or single words in bold type that can be clearly seen from the back row.

The use of color can greatly enhance your visuals. Colors can be particularly useful for highlighting key points.

Explain exactly what each visual means so the audience doesn't have to guess. Even if it's fairly obvious what's on the chart, it is a good habit to repeat it verbally, thus adding reinforcement to the visual key points.

Whenever possible, use your hand to point to visuals. Many speakers misuse pointers, especially the laser kind. Have you ever noticed how distracting it is when a speaker plays with the pointer?

When you've finished with your visual, cover it up, otherwise it will distract the audience from what you're saying. This is particularly true if you're using overhead transparencies; in those cases, turn the light out. If you're using a computer-generated slide presentation, just move it ahead.

Audio Preparation: the Voice

A person knowing the power of his word
becomes very careful in his conversation.
He only has to watch the reactions to his words
to know that they do not return void.
—Florence Scovel Shinn

Your voice is your most powerful tool when presenting, yet many of us are not aware of the sound we make. In order to increase your awareness, make a recording of your presentation and then play it back. Identify the following:

1. **Breath:** do you run out, or do you sound tight, as if you are holding it in?

2. **Pace:** does it stay the same or does it vary?

3. **Pitch:** are you stuck in one tonal range?

4. **Volume:** do you speak too loudly or too softly?

5. **Quality:** does your voice sound thin or does it sound rich and vibrant?

6. **'Um's and 'Ah's:** do you use them instead of just pausing?

Your breath is the power source for your voice. How freely you inhale and exhale dramatically affects the sound of your voice! Learning to use the diaphragm in a natural way is very important. Most vocal problems can be traced back to improper breathing.

Use your voice like an instrument. The only muscle that is involved in producing your voice is the diaphragm. It is the accelerator that regulates the speed and amount of air you put behind your voice.

There are three ways to vary your voice:

- **Loud and soft:** How much breath you inhale and how much you exhale determines the volume. To speak louder, exhale more fully as you speak. To speak softly, exhale slowly and with more control. Allow your diaphragm to be the accelerator and power that determine the amount and speed to put behind your voice.

- **High and low:** Pitch helps create the richness and variety of a voice. Higher-pitched sounds are usually the result of excitement or enthusiasm. To produce lower tones, inhale deeply and, when you exhale, allow the air to flow freely from your chest cavity. It is the air vibrating freely in your chest cavity that produces deep, rich tones.

- **Fast and slow:** Another way to increase variety in your presentation is to play with the rhythm. Speak quickly to increase excitement, pause for dramatic emphasis, and then speak slowly to make your point.

Regularly practicing the 'When I Access Enthusiasm' exercise will help you reduce tension which interferes with breathing. If you want to become a professional presenter, I suggest a few sessions with a voice coach to assist you in the development of your voice.

Microphones and Equipment

Microphones are usually counter-productive for small groups. They cause the speaker to talk in an amplified monotone and can put your audience to sleep. You're better off using your own vocal power if you can make yourself heard at the back of the room. Without a mike, you'll try harder, you'll have better inflection and the audience will listen more carefully.

Some points to remember:

- If your room does require amplification in order for you to be heard, have the sound system adjusted so that you can speak with as much of your own volume as possible.

- If you are using a projector with any regularity, remember Murphy's Law. Expect trouble. Sooner or later a bulb will go out, a slide will get stuck, a computer will shut down, or an LCD will lose its power. If it's an important presentation, bring two of everything. Be prepared for the unexpected.

- If you don't have to turn the house lights all the way down, don't. Keep the room lit as much as possible so you can see your audience and they can see you. Usually darkened rooms are an invitation to drowsiness—especially after lunch.

- Overhead projectors are the most commonly used type of equipment in North American business. They are also the most abused, mainly because the easy-to-make typewritten transparencies can be prepared by anybody, and usually they're only legible to the first two rows of your audience. As a rule of thumb, if you're using an overhead transparency, use a minimum of 14-point type, and add color if you can (i.e. by using a color printer) or use illustrations. Use fewer words—just the highlights. Most of the presentation software programs allow you to design the background and color of your overhead. You can then take it on a disk to a printing/photocopying shop that can print it in color for you. You can also e-mail the material to many of these service centers.

- The next most popular medium is the liquid crystal display projector. This is significantly better than an overhead projector as it can be connected to your computer to display your slides or images. This has several advantages, once you get to know the program. The biggest advantage is ease of use, which saves you time.

- Once you have created a presentation, it can be easily adapted for different audiences. The range of effects can be quite dazzling, so be careful not to overdo it, as this can distract your audience from your message. Take a class in the use of your program. The presentation program and the LCD unit do not replace your skill, or make up for any shortcomings in your presentation. In fact, it will showcase you, good or bad. Using these tools will give the audience the impression that you are up to date with technology, and they will expect you to deliver on that promise.

- You are the audio-visual that is most visible. Tools alone will not impress the audience; they have already sat through too many boring, over-produced, computer-generated presentations. Many speakers think they can use a software program after only ten-to-twenty minutes' preparation. But if you want to be effective and connect with the audience, learn to use the program properly and use it for rehearsal and design, then take a workshop on presentation skills.

- Don't compete. If you are going to use a professionally produced audio-visual module for a change of pace, your best bet is a VHS tape—preferably no longer than seven minutes. Audiences currently perceive VHS videotape as more authoritative or somehow better than slides with sound. When asked to guess the length of business films or tapes, the average person guesses double the actual viewing time. Often the best option is to close with a video presentation, since they are usually so good you cannot compete.

The Importance of Appearance

Whoever I am and whatever I am doing,
some kind of excellence is within my reach.
—John W. Gardener

Know your audience and adjust your appearance accordingly. Keep your suit jacket buttoned during your presentation and you will automatically look more businesslike. Leave your jacket unbuttoned and you'll automatically look more casual. Neither look is 'right' or 'wrong;' it simply depends upon your audience and your environment. Either way you'll be making a definite statement about your attitude towards subject matter and audience. For example, in a retreat setting where it's informal, be relaxed. Where it is more formal, and particularly if it's a first-time business presentation, be more businesslike.

Flashy or noticeable personal accessories, such as jewelry and wristwatches, can be distracting to your listeners. In a presentation setting, less is more. Keep your accessories in your briefcase until after the presentation, if you're in any doubt about their effect on your audience.

Tinted prescription eyeglasses make it difficult for people to make good eye contact with you. Avoid using them when you're speaking to more than thirty people. Audiences desire eye contact!

On-camera Techniques

If your presentation is being videotaped before a live audience, ignore the camera. Likewise, if you're being interviewed before a camera, remember that the video viewer expects to see you communicating with your live audience or the interviewer, not the camera.

If a television reporter is interviewing you, keep your comments short and to the point. TV stations have a nasty habit of editing, sometimes to the point of distorting your statements. Your best defense is to keep it short, clear, and simple.

When you go to a TV studio to be interviewed on television, and they offer you make-up, accept it. The purpose of the make-up is to eliminate glare and give you a more natural look. They usually know what they're doing.

When you perspire under strong TV lights, wipe any obvious perspiration off immediately before you go on the air and again during breaks. Keep tissues in your pocket or very close by. Sweat beading on your forehead or on your lip will make you appear apprehensive, frightened and insincere. If it is a serious problem, get a can of aerosol antiperspirant, spray it on a tissue, and dab it on the areas where you bead sweat.

If you face a hostile interview on camera, avoid looking surprised. Don't pretend that you don't know why you are there. The only preparation is to expect questions like this and not let them lead you into unwarranted confessions, admissions or explanations. Don't act guilty, otherwise the audience will assume you *are* guilty, even if you are not.

Presentation Checklist: a road warrior's experience

When I went to Australia in 1979 on a speaking tour, I made a classic assumption regarding equipment and logistics. I had been spoiled, accustomed to working with a very professional team, and I assumed that everyone knew about this stuff! Australia had a very different system for audio-visuals, different electrical voltage, and different computer programs. What was fortunate for me was the resourcefulness of the sponsors, who were used to North Americans and their assumptions.

I related my experience to a friend who was a pilot, and he suggested developing a checklist so that I would not experience that degree of anxiety and chaos before I got up to make my presentation. I decided that if this approach worked for a professional pilot, it would probably also help me.

The following checklist will help insure the success of your presentations. It is extremely helpful to go through this list several days beforehand. As you do more presentations, you may find it useful to specifically tailor it to your needs. You may also want to consider sending part of this list to the meeting planner at the facility where you are making your presentation. Leave one checklist with the equipment, and fax one ahead to whoever is organizing or sponsoring the event, noting what you will bring and what they are required to provide. Keep one list with you so that you can check it off upon arrival. It is advisable to keep it on your person, together with copies of any computer-software-generated presentations, just in case your briefcase/suitcase gets lost!

Be prepared to succeed, or be prepared for stress.

Checklist

Facilities

_____ Whom to call for help and the phone number (office, mobile)

_____ Restroom location

_____ Phone location

_____ Snack location

_____ Stairs/elevator location

_____ Fire alarm procedures

_____ Signs for directions to meeting

_____ Parking facilities/accommodation

_____ Location of photocopying machine

_____ Phone number for messages

Room

_____ Check light controls and set level

_____ Temperature controls

_____ Disconnect phone in room

_____ Smokers' needs

_____ Chairs/table arrangement

_____ Extension cord

_____ Pencil sharpener

_____ Electrical cords taped down

_____ Coat rack

_____ Lectern

_____ Water pitcher and glasses

_____ Location of electrical outlets

_____ Adapter plug: two-prong or three-prong

_____ Position of spotlights

Overhead Projector/Slide Projector

_____ Spare bulb

_____ Focused

_____ Tray cued to slot one

_____ Opaque slide in slot one

Movie Projector

_____ Film cued up to title frame

_____ Check bulb

_____ Focused and set to fill screen

_____ Sound level check

Music

_____ Cued

_____ Sound level check

Screen

_____ Location

_____ Size

Flip chart

_____ Paper supply

_____ Magic markers

_____ Check for dry ink in markers

Videotape

_____ Check control

_____ Tape cued

_____ Sound level set

Computer-Driven Visuals
_____ Arrive an hour early
_____ Technician on standby
_____ Back-up or bypass alternatives

Microphones
_____ Lavaliere attachment
_____ Extra cord length for movement
_____ Sound check
_____ Back-up mike

Chalk Board
_____ Chalk
_____ Eraser
_____ Clean board

Audience Supplies
_____ Note pads
_____ Pencils
_____ Handouts
_____ Placement cards
_____ Badges
_____ Roster for presenter/participants
_____ Agenda
_____ Table for supplies

Refreshments
_____ Coffee
_____ Decaffeinated
_____ Tea
_____ Juice
_____ Soft drinks
_____ Water/Other

Final Mini-Rehearsal
_____ Opening
_____ Sequence check
_____ Conclusion

After completing several presentations, you will have a good idea of what you require. At that point, you can customize your list. Good preparation will decrease the amount of stress involved, and allow you more energy to be yourself.

Have some fun and get great results.

Room Set-Up

Arrive early and check out the room set-up. Most convention facilities will make the extra effort to rearrange the set-up to suit your needs. Better still, fax in advance the set-up you would prefer. Be ready for last-minute changes to your plans. If you are going to a client's facility, ask about the room layout in advance, and request your preferred set-up so that you can deliver a top-quality presentation.

③ **The Arrow**

A big tough Samurai once went to see a little monk. "Monk," he said, in a voice accustomed to instant obedience, "teach me about heaven and hell!" The monk looked up at this mighty warrior and replied with disdain, "Teach you about heaven and hell? I couldn't teach you about anything. You're dirty. You smell. Your blade is rusty. You're a disgrace, and an embarrassment to the Samurai class. Get out of my sight. I can't stand you." ▷

*The Samurai was furious. He shook, got all red
in the face, and was speechless with rage.
He pulled out his sword and raised it above
him, preparing to slay the monk.*

*"That's hell," said the monk softly.
The Samurai was instantly overwhelmed by the
compassion and surrender of this little man
who had offered his life in order to give this
teaching and show him hell! He slowly put
down his sword, filled with gratitude, and
suddenly peaceful.*

"And that is heaven," said the monk softly.

—Zen saying

The Arrow

> *If you abandon all restraint, carry your wishes*
> *to their furthest limits, open your heart bound-*
> *lessly, there is not a single moment when you*
> *will not find all you could possibly desire.*
> *The present moment holds infinite riches*
> *beyond your wildest dreams.*
> —Jean-Pierre de Caussade

The Arrow represents the message or information to be delivered to the audience.

In order for the arrow to successfully hit the target, it must reflect the conditions in which it is to be used. If we look at the different bows and arrows used in archery for different conditions, we realize that the arrow has to be chosen very carefully.

In medieval times, when the bow and arrow were commonly used, arrows were always made according to the requirements of the archer. The size of the archer and type of bow, and the conditions of its intended use, i.e. the battle field, hunting on foot or on horseback, for practice, for wet or dry weather, or for field competition, were taken into account.

In today's fast-paced world, we often believe that one message (arrow) will work for most audiences. Nothing could be further from the truth. The vast diversity of our society has led to a need for every point of view to be included and recognized.

This represents an enormous challenge for the modern presenter as he/she has to adapt to the specific needs and interests of every audience. The material must be relevant to that audience, and presented in the form of a story, whether it is sixty minutes, six minutes or sixty seconds long.

When you're preparing your talk, begin by outlining your closing remarks, using your last sentence first. This is the last thing they'll hear and the part they're most likely to remember. Many successful trial lawyers use this technique: they write their final argument first and then line up the evidence that best supports their case.

Keeping your Eye on the Target

> *In the long run,*
> *men only hit what they aim at.*
> —Henry David Thoreau

In the process of writing an outline for a presentation, the desired outcome is often lost in the stress of the moment. The following questions are designed to help you see the target more clearly and focus on the needs of the audience:

- Who am I?
- What do I stand for?
- Why am I here today?
- Who is my audience?
- What is their relationship with me?
- What are the content expectations?
- What assumptions do I have?
- Does the topic fit the audience?
- Why is the audience there?
- What do they want to learn?
- How much do they already know?
- What do I want them to know (background, immediate situation, and future)?

- What will make it easy for the audience to understand?
- Do I need visuals and/or written support, other speakers' endorsement(s), research papers or studies?

If you are going to use a professional script or presentation writer, a word of caution: many will have their own understanding of your message. Do not let them take over; their job is to assist you, not replace you. Set the objectives in advance and ask for a budget. Building a presentation is a little like custom-building a house; if you keep changing things, it will be expensive and not what you want. Develop your plan first and stick to it. You are the expert on your message.

Building the Arrow: presentation script writing

Proper organization of your material helps the audience understand your ideas. An oral presentation containing the best material and the most convincing arguments may fail if it is not well organized. Even the most forceful personality may fail to convince his/her audience if his/her material is disorderly. To build an informative and persuasive presentation, you should help your listeners by providing them with guidelines.

The steps involved in presentation script writing can be broken down using the analogy of building an arrow. Each part is important and serves a specific function:

A1: The sharp edge of the Arrowhead is represented by your 'Bio-pic'—your own biographical story. The purpose of the Bio-pic is to create trust and rapport with the NuAudience (the sophisticated, demanding audience of today) so that the arrowhead cleaves through to the Target effectively.

A2: The Arrowhead provides the substance of the presentation. In the Arrowhead, the subject and the purpose of the presentation are explained. This is where you capture your audience's attention, make an impact and give them an overview of your topic.

A3: The Shaft provides the strength and flexibility for the presentation. In the Shaft, the major and minor ideas are developed. Logic is the strength of the shaft. You amplify and simplify these ideas with appropriate visual aids.

A4: The Fletch or Feathers provide stability for the flight of the presentation. In the 'Fletch' stage, you can summarize and leave your audience with a definite, concise impression of what is expected of them. The question-and-answer process also guides the arrow to the desired outcome.

Using this structure to build your script, you will have an excellent outline with which to practice your presentation.

A1: The Bio-pic

The purpose of the Bio-pic (your 'biographical picture') is to give sharpness to the Arrowhead so that it will cleave through to the Target more effectively.

Sharing your own biographical story is a means of enhancing the strength of your message, and is a way of establishing rapport. The key point is that the audience of today is very sophisticated and cynical. Any attempt to deliberately mislead them will ultimately produce negative results. The audience is interested in your values and what your actions represent.

They judge what you do and what you have done, and they listen clearly to what you say and how you say it.

> **Bio-pic: Introduction of self**
>
> **Ideal length: Two minutes or less**
>
> **Subject: YOU**

Most of us are not used to introducing ourselves. Usually someone else does it. But the NuAudience requires much more than that: they want to know who you are, what you stand for and why you are you, relative to the subject matter you are about to address.

Every audience has some emotional connection with the subject or concept that you are going to present. Seek to understand them so that you can communicate effectively. Always consider to whom you are talking and what you are speaking about. Ask yourself what you think your listeners would want to know about you. To prepare for this, the simplest strategy is to ask either the organizer of the event or some of the attendees what they would like to know about you, the presenter, and what they understand or believe about the topic you are presenting.

The purpose of your introduction is to enable you to show up and be heard by your audience so that you can be more effective in all other areas of your presentation.

Here are some questions to stimulate your thinking as you write your Bio-pic for the NuAudience:

- Why are you qualified to speak on this subject?
- What are your responsibilities?

- What do you stand for?
- How does your job fit your talents and personality?
- How has your background prepared you for this position?
- What are your plans and dreams for the future?
- How has your family influenced you?
- What can you tell us about you that will assist us in understanding you?
- What is your vision and overall purpose?
- Why should I listen to you?
- Why do you do what you do?

Take some time to reflect on what you would want an unfamiliar audience to know about you. Unless you give them the necessary information, they will create it in their imagination. This is not meant to be a life story—just enough information for you to connect with the audience.

A2: The Arrowhead

In the Arrowhead, you capture your audience's attention and try to set the mood for your entire presentation. This is critical because, in these few brief moments, you create an atmosphere that could substantially affect the final outcome.

Our research indicates that you have three-to-five minutes in which to create trust and rapport with the audience. Once that time has lapsed, the audience will have made an assessment of you and will then proceed to rationalize their decision about you throughout the remainder of the presentation. Make sure that the real you shows up.

Choose one of the following opening methods to capture the attention of your audience. Based on the exercise in the Archer section, make sure your choice closely reflects your natural style.

1. Ask a series of questions.
2. Tell a human-interest story.
3. Open with a striking quotation.
4. Start with a startling statement.
5. Show an interesting exhibit, chart, or object.
6. Give a specific illustration or graphic description.
7. Refer to the special interests of the audience or the occasion.

After one or more of the seven opening ideas have been used, you must discuss the following points, which make up your opening remarks:

1. Identify the subject you are speaking on.
2. State the purpose of the presentation.
3. Acknowledge the importance of the presentation (if necessary).
4. Outline the main points to be discussed.
5. Indicate the approximate length of your presentation.

A3: The Arrow Shaft

The strength of your presentation lies in the Shaft. This is where you discuss the major and minor points of your presentation. Logic provides the structure for this part of your presentation. In order to present your material in the most effective manner, choose one of the following ten approaches to organizational structure:

1. Subject matter (topic)
2. Problem and solution
3. Cause and effect
4. General to specific
5. Comparison and contrast
6. Familiar to unfamiliar
7. Chronological (time sequence)
8. Advantages and disadvantages
9. Simple to complex
10. Who, what, why, when, where, and how

Cover only the essential points. Ask yourself what information is necessary for your audience to have at this time (remembering the 10% rule). Always present your main or strongest point first.

Include the benefits and reasons why the audience should accept the ideas, plans or products presented. Remember: the audience is always thinking, "What's in it for me?"

When writing your presentation, put yourself in the audience's shoes and list some of the possible benefits for them if they were to take action based on your point of view. However, make sure that the benefits are real and tangible, and based on the true outcome of your point of view.

Potential benefits might include an improvement or increase in one or more of the following: availability, efficiency, performance, uniqueness, reliability, convenience, maintenance, cost, profit, safety, status, beauty, comfort, size, quality, utility, strength, schedule, goodwill, service, compactness, lightness, quantity, weight, and speed.

Use evidence to substantiate any claims that you make. Any of the following approaches can be used:

- Analogies
- Demonstrations
- Examples (case histories)
- Exhibits
- Testimonials
- Facts
- Statistics

Use appropriate language and define any technical terms if you feel the audience will not understand. Never assume that the audience understands your technical language. Avoid the use of slang and trite expressions. Speak *to* the audience, not above or below their intelligence level.

Use stories, anecdotes and illustrations to enliven your presentation and help your listeners remember the points discussed.

Quote authorities on the subject. Be definite and name the person. Also quote popular personalities or a local authority, if possible.

Remember to research the environment in which you will be presenting, and choose the visual aid most appropriate for the occasion. Some visuals will illustrate your points better than others. Often a combination of visual aids is ideal. Investigate the use of large flip charts, desktop flip charts, slides, transparencies, LCD projectors, actual models and the chalkboard.

A4: The Fletch

In any oral presentation, understanding what you want to have happen is the most critical part. Write your last sentence first, so that it will keep you focused on the Target.

A1: Your Bio-pic helped establish trust and rapport with the audience.

A2: Your opening remarks gave the audience the general theme of your presentation.

A3: The Shaft detailed the major and minor points of your material.

A4: The Fletch guides your material to the Target, like the feathers on an arrow. At this point, your audience has a definite picture of the action you wish them to take. As you wrap it up, be careful not to make it too short or abrupt, or too long and tiresome.

Do not add new facts. This is usually a summing-up process to crystallize the audience's thinking. Always leave the audience feeling that you have completed your material on time and with sufficient detail. Get to the point. Wrap it up in such a manner that the audience feels you have stated your position clearly, concisely, and to the point. Use one of the following transition words or phrases to lead you naturally to your conclusion:

- To wrap it up...
- To review...
- In summary...

- Therefore…
- So…
- Remember…
- As I promised…

Always summarize your central theme, and repeat your key points (bearing in mind that the audience will never remember more than three key points). Don't sit down until you've told the audience what you want them to do. Presumably you weren't just talking to be nice, so tell them specifically what you want them to do. If you are just talking to be nice, you are giving a social talk, even if it's to a business audience. In this case, simply end with a pleasant remark.

The most welcome closing for the average business audience is one that comes ahead of schedule. But don't rush to finish early. Plan in advance to do so—if possible, ending five-to-ten minutes early. If you go more than ten minutes past your ending, you're in serious danger of losing your listeners. To avoid this, break down your presentation into modules or digestible bits of ten-to-twelve minutes, each with their own single key point.

If you plan to move into a question-and-answer period after your presentation, the transition will be your closing period rather than a chronological ending. Therefore plan for a logical conclusion before you accept questions and save a minute or two at the end of the question period for a brief recap.

Bring back your best visual to accompany your closing remarks. This will give your audience both verbal and visual reinforcement of your central theme. Of course, knowing in advance that you're going to return to the key visual will also keep you focused on your closing remarks during the entire presentation.

Here are four closing strategies:

1. **Appeal** for specific action by the audience;
2. **Read** an appropriate quotation or quote an authority;
3. **Quote** a fitting verse of poetry;
4. **Use** a humorous close but, in this age of political correctness, you need to be aware of the sensibilities of the audience. The best form of humor is a personal anecdote or story.

Question-and-Answer Period

One of the most effective ways of closing a presentation is to hold a question-and-answer period. This allows you to assess the audience's understanding of what you have presented and allows you to clarify and make the specific points you suspect have been lost.

Sometimes the hardest part of a Q&A period is getting people to ask questions. This is especially true with large audiences because no one wants to be first. Try to break the ice by asking easy, conversational questions related to your subject. Once the first person speaks, the questions will follow.

Unless you want to be interrupted in the middle of your talk, let the audience know in advance that you're saving plenty of time for questions at the end, and ask them to hold their questions until that time.

With audiences of thirty or more people, it's a good idea to repeat each question so the entire audience knows exactly what you've been asked. This also gives you valuable thinking time. You don't have to repeat each question verbatim; just make sure you re-state the essential elements.

Do not change the contextual or emotional meaning of a question asked.

Look directly at the person asking you a question and make sure they're finished before you start your answer. During your answer, don't look at the questioner, but talk to the rest of the audience. If you direct your attention only to the questioner, you'll lose the audience's attention.

Don't return to the person who asked the question to ask them if you've answered their question. You may not have, but the rest of the audience may not care, so avoid starting a detailed discussion with one person. Keep it moving and go on to the next question.

If a previous questioner comes back for a more thorough answer, and it happens to be your boss, you know what to do! If it's a nitpicker, be polite; give some additional information, but don't get bogged down. If he or she persists, tell them you'll be happy to meet with them afterwards for a longer discussion of that specific point.

Let the audience know when you're wrapping it up by announcing that you have time for only one more question. Be specific; if you intend to take two or more, tell them, but avoid saying "one or two more" as it sounds indecisive.

Proper strategy on your part will help you decide whether to do this immediately afterwards or whether you will answer questions during your presentation. If you have sufficient time (more than ninety minutes), handling questions during your presentation would be the ideal plan. If you are unfamiliar with the material, unprepared, or have a hostile audience, it would be better to have the question-and-answer period at the end. This enables you to complete your presentation without interruption or heckling.

Give considerable thought to your closing remarks so that you can finish your presentation confidently, correctly, and with the results you desire.

Re-state your closing remarks after the question-and-answer period.

Effectively Handling Questions

Here are some general guidelines for effectively handling questions. Always respect your audience in this process, bearing in mind that everyone has his/her point of view. If you become defensive, you will lose the respect and confidence of your audience.

Don't:
- argue; you will lose the audience
- posture or pout
- imply with body language, "What a stupid question"
- say, "Good question"
- unnecessarily repeat the question
- change your style

Do:
- encourage questions, lean forward and indicate by body language that you are interested
- listen to and look directly at the questioner, but present your answer to everyone
- use the question to reinforce your point of view
- be brief and friendly

The 10% Rule: less is more effective

Use only 10% of your available information. The other 90% is for your 'ground,' and to enhance your confidence, increase your focus, and help refine the structure of your presentation. It is to provide weight and stability for you, the presenter, increasing your self-confidence and strengthening your position at the front of the room.

What the audience needs to know: 10%

Your knowledge: 90%

Like an iceberg, let only 10% of your knowledge show. Focus on the specific needs of your audience, and ask yourself what they need to hear. The NuAudience wants to know what you believe is relevant, but not everything that you know. Less is more. Many presenters over-prepare their material, providing too much information for the listener to absorb.

This is usually due to three things:

1. The presenter's lack of understanding of the audience.
2. His/her lack of focus and structure.
3. His/her lack of confidence.

④ The Target

Once there was a disciple of a Greek philosopher who was commanded by his Master to give money to everyone who insulted him. When this period of trial was over, the Master said to him, "Now you can go to Athens and learn wisdom."

When the disciple was entering Athens, he saw a wise man sitting at the gate, insulting everybody who came and went. He also insulted the disciple, who immediately burst out laughing.

"Why do you laugh when I insult you?" said the wise man. "Because," said the disciple, "for three years I have been paying for this kind of thing and now you give it away for nothing."

"Enter the city," said the wise man. "It is all yours."

—an Arab saying

The Target

Talking of bulls is not the same
as being in the bullring.
—Spanish saying

The Target represents the audience, which, for the presenter, is the most important element. The audience pre-selects the type of event that they wish to attend, whether for business, education or some other purpose. As a presenter, you need to know as much as possible about your audience.

The discriminating modern audience—the NuAudience—will forgive hesitation, nervousness, and technical glitches, but will never forgive disrespect or arrogance on the part of the speaker. Trying to show off, winging it, and pretending familiarity or a depth-of-knowledge you don't possess, all show disrespect for your audience. It also indicates a great deal of arrogance on the part of the speaker if he/she believes that, in this day of sophistication, the NuAudience can be so easily duped.

The NuAudience expects and demands more, having seen in person or on videotape some of the world's best speakers. Although they do not expect you to match that level of performance, they do expect you to bring the one thing all of theses speakers have in common—authentic self-expression. The NuAudience has 'been there, done that,' and has a high degree of cynicism, which can only be overcome with sincerity and competence on the part of the speaker.

Listening Habits

> *If the doors of perception were cleansed,*
> *everything would appear to man*
> *as it is—infinite.*
>
> —William Blake

No one is born with the ability to listen effectively. Just like all other communication skills, good listening must be *learned*. To a great extent, this involves breaking old habits and forming new ones. Here is a short test, which, if *answered honestly*, will give you an idea of whether your listening habits could be improved. It will also give you a better understanding of your audience, as a result of putting yourself in their place.

Please answer YES/NO.

1. You think about four times faster than a person usually talks. Do you use this excess time to think about other things while you're keeping track of the conversation?   Y/N

2. Do you listen primarily for facts, rather than ideas, when someone is speaking?   Y/N

3. Do you avoid listening to things you feel will be too difficult to understand?   Y/N

4. Can you tell from a person's appearance and delivery whether they will have anything worthwhile to say?   Y/N

5. When somebody is talking to you, do you try to make him/her think you're paying attention when you're not?   Y/N

6. Do certain words or phrases prejudice you so that you cannot listen objectively?   Y/N

7. Do you turn your thoughts to other subjects when you believe a speaker will have nothing particularly interesting to say?   Y/N

8. When you're listening to someone, are you easily distracted by outside sights and sounds?   Y/N

9. When you are puzzled or annoyed by what someone says, do you try to get the question straightened out immediately, either in your own mind or by interrupting the speaker?   Y/N

10. In a conversation, do you catch yourself concentrating more on what you are going to say when it's your turn to speak, than on what the speaker is saying?   Y/N

If you truthfully answered "NO" to all the questions, you are a rare individual—perhaps a perfect listener. (You may also be kidding yourself!) Every "YES" means you have a habit that impairs your ability to listen and communicate effectively—and therefore to successfully communicate at the front of the room.

Today's Business World

*The rich substance of the universe is yours to do
with as you wish. Why settle for so little in life
when you can have so much, just by daring to
be different in your thinking.*
— Catherine Ponder, *Dare to Prosper*

The business world of the next millennium will be quite different to that of today, as will be the consumer! In the 1960s, competition was not as intense, the role of women was different, and consumer expectations were not as high. The corporate management model was hierarchical, with the average employee's education being less advanced than it is today. The social and technological revolution had just begun, and it is speeding up as we approach the year 2000.

This new business world requires that we present and sell our ideas not only to our customers, but also to our staff. Today, we make presentations all the time, via voice mail, e-mail, in staff meetings, sales meetings, planning sessions, and to outside agencies, special interest groups, unions, and government agencies, all before we even get to the customer.

The kinds of presentations we make have changed from the authoritarian directive to the casual, informative style, and from the aggressive or pushy sales style, to the team-player relationship approach. And the success of these presentations has a significant impact on the future of your company.

To effectively reach and inspire the NuAudience, values-based communication and authenticity are essential. To ignore the trends of this NuAudience (the way they think and their high level of awareness and discernment) can spell disaster for the presenter. If ill prepared for communicating with this audience, the presenter will lack the ground necessary to be effective.

Trends of the NuAudience

> *You get people to do what you want*
> *not by bullying them or tricking them,*
> *but by understanding them.*
>
> —Raven

The NuAudience is made up of independent thinkers who seek control over their lives. This group has seen the Vietnam War, Watergate and Nixon's resignation, various stock market swindles, the rise and fall and rise of Apple (Steve Jobs), the rise of Microsoft (Bill Gates), the Gulf War, and the Bill and Monica scandal. They have seen senators resigning their positions before the onslaught of public scrutiny (in both the US and Canada), and a former Prime Minister investigated for bribery by the incoming government. The NuAudience has become very skeptical about trusting elected officials and has a high degree of cynicism as a result.

The members of this audience are more educated and sophisticated, with more post-secondary education than any other generation before them. Most have had two distinct careers, or two functions within the same career. They know how to find out what is going on, and to access information once reserved for a select few. They ask questions, and expect to get the answers.

They seek a higher quality of life. They have had bigger and more, and now they want better quality, and less stress in the process, and are willing to pay for it. They are interested in spiritual growth and its application in their day-to-day lives.

They are extremely demanding, and becoming less tolerant of poor service. The NuAudience is aware of consumer power and how to use it. With consumer advocacy on the rise, and various media outlets reporting on individuals who have been 'cheated,' this trend will only grow. Ellen Phillips' new book, *Shocked, Appalled and Dismayed: How to Write Letters of Complaint that Get Results,* is a great example of how this NuAudience deals with problems. They will no longer just sit and take it. They won't get mad; they'll just let you and everyone else know about it.

Optimistic, but well grounded in reality, they have had boom times and hard times and will work to create the best for themselves again. They will support businesses and governments that help them, however security is becoming more of an issue as they age. They are planning for their retirement, and want to be self-supporting, while retaining their independence and lifestyle.

They seek new experiences and innovation. The NuAudience is part of the group for whom 'sex, drugs and rock 'n' roll' was a truism, but now they take yoga and meditation classes. They started on Macintosh computers and have graduated to 300mhz-plus PCs. They've gone from five-channel TV to the 100-channel universe. And from the Detroit Big Three auto-makers, they've expanded their options to include some 15 international auto-makers, each with many vehicles and options.

Aging but still active, this group started jogging and participating in marathons and triathlons. They continue to defy previously known limits concerning age and stamina. If anyone can rewrite the book on aging, this group can. They continue to experiment with nutrition, vitamins, hormones and various life-extending combinations.

Pursuers of wellness, they are proactive in resolving their own health concerns as well as those of their families. Many have become vegetarian. They have taken a serious, critical look at the issue of health and health providers, creating the current explosion in alternative medicine. For the first time, the sanctified position of the medical community, and the powerful influence of the pharmaceutical industry are under intense scrutiny, and the tools being used are freedom of information and access to the Internet. Members of the NuAudience can now research medical reports and studies directly, without the interpretation or censorship of the mainstream healthcare industry.

They are increasingly proactive in environmentalism. The logging interests of British Columbia ignored them and paid a high price in terms of public support, not only in BC but also outside Canada. In the now-famous Clayoquot Sound confrontation between MacMillan Bloedel (a forestry giant) and Greenpeace (a largely volunteer environmental activist organization), Greenpeace gained the upper hand because the group understood the NuAudience. Greenpeace used its huge and well-politicized European influence and connections to pressure MacMillan Bloedel into changing their forestry practices. With the potential for economic losses, MacMillan Bloedel realized that they could not win and opted instead to become part of this new trend. They brought in a new president, who subsequently issued a moratorium on clear-cutting and began working with Greenpeace.

Often organizations and individuals hold onto what they know, creating problems for themselves because of their inflexibility towards change, in a world where change can happen overnight. The forestry industry of BC has, in the past, stubbornly ignored the very obvious changes taking place. Now, due to public pressure and economic necessity, they are being forced to change.

The NuAudience is far less homogeneous. At one time in North America, you could have described the political parties as Republican, Democrat, NDP, Conservative and Liberal, and had a fairly good idea of what these different parties represented. Today we have the right wing or left wing of all parties, tremendous overlap on issues, and conflict about what they represent. Now, rather than being loyal to any one party, the NuAudience is motivated more by specific issues and values which they deem important.

Dr Ray, a demographer in the US, has also defined this group. He calls them 'Cultural Creatives.' According to Dr Ray, they are well-employed, middle-to-upper class, professional, well-educated, highly-paid, and tend to live in the western and coastal regions of North America. They are thirty-to-fifty-five years old. In 1980, they represented 4% of the US population. Today they account for 24%. This is a significant change—a "shift in the dominant culture pattern which," says Dr Ray, "occurs only once or twice in a millennium."

Factors that Influence the NuAudience

Each year, the staff at Beloit College in Wisconsin puts together a list of factors that provides their faculty with a sense of the mindset of that year's incoming freshmen.

These factors reflect the emerging NuAudience, what they have experienced, what their point of reference is, and what has influenced them. This cultural background also indicates how they make decisions.

Here is the College's list for 1999:

1. The people who are starting college this fall across the nation were born in 1980.

2. They have no meaningful recollection of the Reagan Era and did not know he had ever been shot.

3. They were pre-pubescent when the Persian Gulf War was waged.

4. Black Monday 1987 is as significant to them as the Great Depression.

5. There has been only one Pope. They can only really remember one president.

6. They were 11 when the Soviet Union broke apart and do not remember the Cold War.

7. They have never feared a nuclear war. *The Day After* is a pill to them, not a movie.

8. They are too young to remember the space shuttle blowing up.

9. Tiananmen Square means nothing to them.

10. Their lifetime has always included AIDS.

11. Bottle caps have always been screw-off and plastic.

12. Atari pre-dates them, as do vinyl albums.

13. The expression, "you sound like a broken record" means nothing to them.

14. They have never owned a record player.

15. They have likely never played Pac Man, and have never heard of Pong.

16. *Star Wars* looks very fake to them, and the special effects are pathetic.

17. There have always been red M&Ms and blue ones are not new. There used to be beige ones?

18. They may have heard of an eight-track, but have probably never actually seen or heard one.

19. The Compact Disc was introduced when they were one year old.

20. As far as they know, stamps have always cost about 32 cents.

21. They have always had an answering machine.

22. Most have never seen a TV set with only thirteen channels, nor have they seen a black-and-white TV.

23. They have always had cable.

24. There have always been VCRs, but they have no idea what a BETA machine is.

25. They cannot fathom not having a remote control.

26. They were born the year that Walkmen were introduced by Sony.

27. Roller-skating has always meant inline for them.

28. *The Tonight Show* has always been with Jay Leno.

29. They have no idea when or why Jordache jeans were cool.

30. Popcorn has always been cooked in the microwave.

31. They have never seen Larry Bird play, and Kareem Abdul-Jabbar is a football player.

32. They never took a swim and thought about *Jaws*.

33. The Vietnam War is as ancient history to them as WWI, WWII or even the Civil War.

34. They have no idea that Americans were ever held hostage in Iran.

35. They can't imagine what hard contact lenses are.

36. They don't know who Mork was or where he was from.

37. They never heard: "Where's the beef?", or "I'd walk a mile for a Camel," or "de plane, de plane!"

38. They do not care who shot J.R. and have no idea who J.R. is.

39. The *Titanic* was found? I thought we always knew where it was.

40. Michael Jackson has always been white.

41. Kansas, Chicago, Boston, America, and Alabama are places, not musical groups.

42. McDonald's never came in styrofoam containers.

43. There has always been MTV.

There is always a NuAudience waiting to listen to you. Do you know what to say?

The NuAudience and Business

> *Change and growth take place*
> *when a person has risked himself,*
> *and dares to become involved*
> *in experimenting with his own life.*
> —Herbert Otto

In today's highly competitive business world, you are always presenting yourself, your product, and your ideas! Yet you cannot assume that the audience knows or understands you, so you need to put yourself in their position and ask yourself some of the questions they would be likely to have. The following questions will help you prepare for your presentation.

Who are you? The NuAudience will want to know what you stand for and why. Although you may never have to actually present this information, it is important to know the answer to this question.

What company do you represent? At one time, you could just say, "I work for IBM" and the listener would have a certain faith in, and understanding of, that statement. But how many computer companies are there today? In early 1999, computer giants Dell and IBM announced a special supply relationship, despite the fact that Dell had been considered a rival of IBM in the PC market place. The whole industry has changed and will continue to do so. Be specific about your company.

What is your company's product or service? With the proliferation of brands and divisions, it is hard to tell who does what. For example, General Motors Corporation has branched into numerous worldwide alliances and products. Honda now builds in North America, blurring the line between what is considered domestic and imported.

What does your company stand for? Today the NuAudience wants to know all the details. With their superior awareness and access to information, they know that one division may be working for the environment, whereas another may be being charged for environmental damage.

What kind of reputation does your company have? Are you prepared to live up to your company reputation? Are you who you say you are? The tobacco industry faces a huge challenge, having to prove that it has not deliberately targeted children in order to create nicotine addiction. The NuAudience will want to know the truth.

Now… what was it you wanted to sell me?

Workforce Attitudes

> *We cannot change the inevitable. The only*
> *thing we can do is play the one string we have,*
> *and that is our attitude. I am convinced that*
> *life is 10% what happens to me and 90%*
> *how I react to it. And so it is with you.*
> *We are in charge of our attitudes.*
>
> —Charles Swindoll

A survey of 2,039 Canadians (the WorkCANADA Survey), carried out by management consulting firm Watson Wyatt Worldwide, revealed that the view from the top of the corporate ladder is often distorted. Senior executives seemed to be more impressed with their own abilities, for example, than were their employees.

As part of the survey, workers were asked to rate whether mangers treated them with respect and dignity. Only 37% of hourly-paid employees said they did, despite the fact that 66% of senior managers claimed to treat people with respect and dignity.

Company employees were also asked if senior management behaved consistently with company values—whether they 'walked the talk.' Only 40% of production workers believed that they did, whereas 64% of managers claimed to do so.

Poor communication skills were also found to be a problem. According to the survey, 61% of senior executives said they were doing a good job of communicating, but only 33% of the managers and department heads agreed.

The communication gap seemed to get wider between management level and those further down the hierarchical ladder: 61% of senior executives said they are doing a good job of communicating, whereas only 22% of professional staff, 27% of clerical workers, and 22% of hourly-paid workers agreed.

I believe that good communication skills are the key to leading a modern company. The old style of command and control ignores the reality of the modern workforce. This is the most educated, mobile and resourceful workforce that has ever been available for hire. Employees today demand respect, they ask why, and make up their own mind. If they are personally motivated, they can produce amazing results.

Just recently, I had a dramatic example of this. A large accounting and consulting firm lost their software-programming group when a senior partner insisted that everyone wear suits and ties to work. A small issue? Obviously not! You do not tell highly-qualified, highly mobile and highly-paid individuals what to wear—at least, not if you understand the NuAudience. They won't take it, don't have to take it and they have the resources to leave. If you take a look at the software and computer industries, you will see that they are not hidebound by the past. Although they are not perfect, they know they must be flexible or they will not succeed.

Any company undergoing change would be well advised to read the WorkCANADA Survey to gain a deeper understanding of the need for change and flexibility in the workplace. (The results of an equivalent study of the United States workforce are also available from Watson Wyatt Worldwide.)

The Halo Effect

Eighty percent of success is just showing up.
—Woody Allen

Our surveys show that within the NuAudience:

30%   admire you, just because you are
speaking, relieved that it is you,
rather than them, speaking at the
front of the room

30%   listen because of interest in the
subject, and admire you because
you are speaking

10%   listen with interest and discernment

30%   are distracted: they have an
internal agenda and so are not
fully available to listen or interact

In our audience surveys, we found that most listeners give the presenter about three-to-five minutes to warm up. After that, their more critical judgement will surface. There is one thing all audiences seem to hate: apathy on the part of the presenter. Demonstrate that you care and they will too; if *you* don't, *they* won't either.

Presentation Research

Always research your audience before deciding on the presentation strategy to use. Below are some questions to stimulate your thinking on this.

Audience

- Who is your audience?
- What is their relationship to you?
- What do they expect from you?
- What assumptions do you have?
- What is their corporate culture?
- What do you know about their personal culture?

Topic

- Is the topic appropriate?
- Why is the audience there?
- What do they want to learn?
- How much do they already know?
- What do you want them to know (background, immediate situation, future, etc)?

Personal Impact

*To have played and laughed with enthusiasm
and sung life's song with joy;
to be happy that even one life has been
enriched because you have lived;
that is to have shown up.*

—Raven

When deciding on the personal impact you wish to make, remember that your appearance does matter. The audience will make judgements about you and the content of your presentation, based on their personal prejudices. Sometimes you may flout convention in order to make a dramatic point, but be sure it really serves you and your message.

Clothing and personal appearance are ways of communicating values, self-image and self-respect. Be aware of the messages you send. Your appearance can create a relaxed, personal environment in which the listener can easily identify with you and make an emotional connection, or it can create a substantial barrier.

Maximize your credibility and authority with a smart-looking first impression. Since all men's and most women's jackets are tailored to be buttoned, I recommend keeping them buttoned to begin with. When the jacket is buttoned, a 'V' is created at the neckline, which draws your listeners' eyes to your face, and helps them focus on your message. If your listeners are less formally dressed, and a more relaxed environment is desirable, you can always unbutton the jacket or take it off.

Choose colors that project how you would like to be perceived. Moods and feelings are inextricably bound to different colors. Harmonious colors are adjacent to each other on the color wheel, whereas contrasting colors are located opposite each other.

To create an authoritative or assertive mood, combine colors such as black, French navy, chocolate brown or charcoal gray with contrasting white shirts and blouses. To soften the mood, soften the contrast. A softer contrast creates a mood that is light and easy—a mood that spells vulnerability, approachability and openness.

If you are uncertain about what looks good on you, hire a wardrobe consultant. It's a fun way to see what works in helping you appear more confident. This is an effective strategy for both men and women.

Eliminating Distractions

Audible distractions are among the most annoying. Before a presentation, always empty your pockets of keys and coins. Be extra careful to remove pagers, cellular phones, etc. Take off bracelets that can jangle and make noise. Keep jewelry to a minimum.

Wear clothes that are the right cut and fit. Don't wear clothes that are too small: it looks unprofessional and you will look heavier. Be comfortable with yourself. You need to be able to button a jacket, and your skirt or pants should not crease excessively. The ideal tie length is down to the middle of the belt buckle.

Be neat. Before a presentation or meeting, look at yourself in a mirror and straighten up your appearance. Make sure pocket flaps are out, tie knots are straight, pant legs are not stuck in your socks, slips aren't showing, and no loose threads are hanging. Anything askew about your dress and appearance is distracting. Making sure you look neat will help eliminate those distractions.

Dress and groom up, not down. As a presenter, it is safer and more comfortable to be slightly overdressed. Do not wear evening clothes, i.e. sheer fabrics, extremely high heels, or elaborate jewelry. Style your hair away from your face. Men with beards or mustaches should make sure they are well groomed and trimmed.

The eyes have it. If you wear glasses, make sure the lenses are clear and clean. Your listeners want to see your facial expressions and focus on your eyes.

The bottom line is to know your audience and dress appropriately. That way you will avoid dressing too casually or too conservatively.

⑤ Practical Strategies

The whole family went out to dinner one evening. Menus were passed to all, including Molly, the eight-year-old daughter. The conversation was an adult one, so Molly was ignored.

When the waiter took orders, he came to Molly last. "And what do you want?" he asked. "A hot dog and a soda," she replied. "No," said her grandmother, "she'll have the roast chicken dinner, with carrots and mashed potatoes." "And milk to drink," chimed in her father.

"Would you like ketchup or mustard on your hotdog?" asked the waiter as he walked away, taking the parents aback. "Ketchup," she called out. She then turned to her family and added, "You know what? He thinks I am real."

—Anonymous

Practical Strategies

If I always do what I have always done,
I will always get what I have always got.

—Anonymous

The following practical strategies are based on my experience, not only as a presenter but also as a coach of other presenters. I call them 'practical' because they concern the act of doing. If you use them long enough—for about thirty days—you will develop a series of good habits that will greatly enhance your presentation skills.

1. **Reduce anxiety by being well prepared.** The number one form of protection against anxiety is knowing your subject matter. Be prepared and you'll naturally feel better about your presentation. Develop your 'ground,' and practice your presentation, applying all the skills you have learned so far. Then use them or lose them. Most individuals put more care, thought and action into planning a vacation than into a presentation that could possibly affect their lives.

2. **Talk to one person at a time.** Literally look directly into the eyes of one listener at a time, just as you would in a normal day-to-day conversation. This might be difficult at first, if you're used to scanning and avoiding eye contact, but it's worth the effort to acquire this basic habit of effective communication. This will help you build rapport and trust with your audience, and it also helps calm anxiety, not only in yourself but also among your listeners.

3. **Stand up straight.** Good posture makes it easier for you to breathe and, in turn, easier for you to get your words out naturally. This helps you build confidence and look natural. Deep breathing before you start calms nerves and provides oxygen to fuel your presentation.

4. **Don't rely on drugs or alcohol to calm your nerves.** The resulting slowed reactions, slurred speech and hazy memory will be counterproductive; they will also create the opportunity for some kind of disaster to happen, and will diminish your professionalism.

5. **Know your opening and closing lines.** Know exactly where you want to go, having written your last sentence first. Practice your opening statement; it'll get you going. Our research shows that you have three-to-five minutes' grace before the critical mind of the audience kicks in.

6. **Hold your position.** Just before you get up to speak, and say to yourself, "I know what I'm going to say, and I'm glad for the chance to say it." The audience has some interest either in you or your subject matter, otherwise they would not be there.

7. **Speak up.** Talk a little louder than you think you have to. Most people speak far too softly and it sounds like they're mumbling. Speaking up also helps you calm any anxiety or nervousness and helps with pronunciation.

8. **Be yourself.** If you're over six feet tall, you do not have the option of speaking softly. Your sound, volume and projection must match your physical appearance. The idea is to

capitalize on your individual uniqueness. We are all physically equipped to sound different, and there is a natural sound for each individual.

9. **Use illustrations.** The listeners' minds are hungry for pictures. Give them something to see. Use analogies and stories so they can visualize along with you. As Confucius said, "A picture is worth a thousand words." I believe this concept should be tempered with the knowledge that you yourself are the most powerful audio-visual. Use audio-visuals to support yourself, but don't let them dominate your presentation.

10. **Use first-person stories whenever possible.** The audience perks up when they hear phrases like, "The other day, I..." or, "I have found from my own experience..." or "A friend of mine once told me..."

11. **Pause occasionally.** Pauses are perhaps the most effective technique for regaining your audience's attention. Most speakers don't use this powerful idea because the silence seems deafening to them. However, the audience welcomes the pause. They usually relax and re-focus. Try it and you'll see all eyes looking back to you for your next statement.

12. **Save handouts until after your presentation.** If you give people material at the beginning of your talk, they'll read it instead of paying attention to you. If you are giving information that requires substantiation for legal or scientific reasons, have the handout ready for the audience and include all the research information. Don't hide anything;

given the resources available to today's audience, you will almost certainly be found out. Hand it out at the end of your presentation, for review later.

13. **Use rhetorical questions** like, "What would you think if…?" You don't expect anyone to answer these questions out loud, but they have the effect of forcing people to respond mentally, hence keeping them on track with you. Ask questions—the kind that you believe your audience would ask. Make sure you have done your audience research first. And don't be afraid of asking and answering the tough questions during your presentation. If you don't, they will, either directly or in their mind.

14. **Show up and you will be heard.** Your personal style of presentation may not be the same as that of anybody you know. There is no prototype of a successful presenter. The measuring stick of a good presenter is always effectiveness based on audience feedback. Do not let an old-style presenter try to make you into a 'perfect' or 'ideal' speaker, as this has the potential to make you sound and look like everyone else. This is about you, so learn to express yourself, through skills and experience. This is a process, not a critiquing event. Authentic self-expression is what the audience asks of you.

15. **Just do it and learn.** Good presentation skills must be developed. Use them or lose them. You may compare making presentations to playing tennis or golf. They're all physical activities and, just like your golf or tennis game, your speaking style will suffer with inactivity. Opportunities for presenting are abundant. Use every chance you have to make a presentation.

16. **Use the words of others.** Become a collector of quotations for use in future talks. Use a 3x5" card file, indexed by subject. If this is too much work, buy a book of quotations.

17. **Make it easy.** Provide your own written introduction. The person introducing you will appreciate it. You can relax, knowing it's accurate and appropriate for your talk.

18. **Avoid sibilance.** Don't drink coffee or soft drinks before speaking. They cause sibilance—hissing sounds—especially with difficult words beginning or ending in 's.' To quench thirst, I recommend Gatorade, which will provide a good combination of fluid and nutrients.

19. **Be prepared.** Carry visual aids prepared in several formats—slides, overheads, flip charts, and floppy disks—so that you'll be prepared for any situation when you travel.

20. **Get fit.** Professional presenters are physically fit and graceful. Try ballroom dancing, aerobics, jogging, boxing or fencing lessons. Get enough sleep and rest, and daydream about your successful presentation. This is good basic training for success.

21. **Think of others.** Practice pronouncing final syllables. Make sure the final consonants are formed distinctly; over-do it. A large percentage of the population has a hearing problem; think of them when you practice.

22. **Acknowledge the question.** When repeating questions during a Q&A session, don't say, "That's a good question." (What you usually mean is, "I've got a good answer.") It

also implies that questions asked by others in the audience were not good. The audience knows that sometimes the question is truly dumb. Say 'I acknowledge your question,' then reply if you can.

23. **Be yourself.** Unless you have an accent that is so pronounced that people actually have difficulty understanding it, don't try to change it. It gives you character and a different quality of sound. You don't have to sound like a network newscaster to be an effective presenter. In fact, a slight accent has a quality of realism and warmth that adds to your credibility and uniqueness.

24. **Change is good.** Professional presenters may give the same talk many times over. To avoid getting so familiar with your material that you run the risk of sounding mechanical and flat, change your stories and illustrations according to the particular needs or interest of your audience.

25. **Let them remember you.** If you want to present like a pro, be authentic. Give your audience something to remember about you.

Accessing your Enthusiasm: a powerful way to be

*Far more people act themselves
into a new way of thinking
than think themselves into a new way of action.*
—Raven

Let your audience know that you're committed to your ideas and that you're excited about them. They'll not only see your enthusiasm, they will feel it and they will get a glimpse of the real you. Enthusiasm is contagious (as is low energy). If it's important enough to talk about, there's room for enthusiasm.

We judge others by their behavior, and we judge ourselves by our intentions. Access your enthusiasm in order for your audience to know how you feel about what you're presenting. They don't know your intentions; they can only judge by your actions and the amount of genuine enthusiasm you show.

One of the most powerful impacts of a presentation filled with sincere enthusiasm is the appreciation, surprise and genuine delight on the faces of your listeners. In today's world of advanced communication technology, there is a renewed demand for old-fashioned, person-to-person connection. Individuals want the personal touch. They want you to speak to them directly and to reach them in some meaningful way. Show up and be heard.

Delivering Text

> *To conquer fear is the beginning of wisdom.*
> —Bertrand Russell

Most speeches that are read word-for-word are painfully boring unless a professional speechwriter or a professional coach has written them. The last time most of us were read to, we fell asleep.

I have seen presidents of major corporations make the mistake of not knowing the material and relying on the staff writer to create their presentation. You can tell when it happens: all of a sudden they abandon the slides or script, and start using their own words. This is an indication that what was written did not match their belief. At one Board of Trade presentation, I watched the president of a learning agency lose his way during the presentation. A staff member was running the Power Point program, and his pace was different to that of the president. The video portion was so dynamic that it flustered the already-overwhelmed and out-paced president. The subsequent feedback about the president was less than complimentary.

If you must read your speech, bear in mind the following points:

- **Be exact.** If every single word of your talk must be exact for legal or technical reasons, have it typed in the largest possible typeface (for example, 14- or 16-point Courier typeface). Have only five or six words per line so you can read it easily without having to keep your eyes glued to the paper, and don't let sentences spill over to the next page.

- **Use gestures.** Use one hand to keep your place in your script, keeping the other hand free for appropriate gestures. Otherwise there's nothing for the audience to watch but a talking head bent slightly forward.

- **Keep your place.** If you lose your place, pause for a second, go back, and repeat the last sentence. (The audience will assume that you're doing it for dramatic effect.)

- **Minimize distractions.** Slide pages to the side as you finish reading them. Turning pages distracts your audience, and acts as a constant reminder that you're reading instead of talking to them.

- **Include the human element.** If possible, even if most of your remarks are read verbatim, try to incorporate at least one incident, illustration or story that you can tell in your own words. Even a few moments of unrehearsed conversation with your audience will break the monotonous and boring spell of reading to them.

- **Stay on time.** The biggest danger in speaking from notes or using an outline is losing track of time. Have you ever noticed how often speakers get carried away with the first point of a five-point talk, and then have to rush to cover other points?

- **Be specific.** Organize your talk around specific examples or evidence that you plan to use, rather than ad-libbing about the topic heading.

- **See clearly.** Print notes or outlines in large letters with colorful felt pens. Even if you wear glasses, you won't have to strain to pick up your next point.

- **Stay on track.** Use one page or individual index cards for each point in your presentation. This will help you stay on track. When you go to the next page or card, pause briefly to give the audience a chance to absorb the information you've just given them.

- **Highlight quotations.** If you're using a direct quotation in your presentation, hold up the card or page you're reading from so that they can see that you're reading. This is the one time that you want to make it clear that you're reading something. It adds authority to the quote. Make it clear that it's a quotation, and specify when it was said and who said it.

- **Trust that you know.** Use short sentences or key words rather than complete sentences to organize your notes. The phrases and key words will serve as memory joggers but won't restrict you to an exact sentence that might not flow naturally in a conversational, live talk.

- **Be visual.** Use a color code such as a red dot to indicate where you plan to introduce a visual. It's a good idea to have a miniature version of your visuals incorporated into your notes so you can introduce them with smooth transitions.

Absolutes and 'No-No's

All urge is blind save when there is knowledge;
and all knowledge is vain save when there is work;
and all work is empty save when there is love.
—Kahlil Gibran, *The Prophet*

Don't ever use off-color material or four-letter words in a business presentation. Even in an all-male gathering, the most masculine speaker can get along without running the risk of sounding unbusinesslike and uncouth. This is not prudish, but rather a basic principle of good business communication. Just because you can swear or tell a joke does not mean that you are a leader who should be listened to.

Don't accept a speaking assignment that you don't have time to prepare for. It's possible to speak on practically any subject if you have time to prepare. But the most disastrous presentations are given by so-called experts who simply are not prepared to speak and haven't done the necessary groundwork. Don't fake it till you make it! This old adage is not valid in this context, and the NuAudience will know that you are faking it. This can have serious consequences for your credibility.

Don't attempt to answer a question if you don't honestly know the answer. Of course, spontaneous answers to routine questions are not expected to be perfect. However, any suggestion of fabrication will destroy a speaker's credibility. When you get a tough question that you can't answer, say so and add confidently that you will get the information to the questioner and anyone else who's interested. For sales and marketing executives, this is a perfect invitation for a follow-up contact. If you have the names and addresses of those in the audience, provide them also with the answers to the questions. This builds credibility and trust for your organization and yourself.

Don't ever lose your temper in front of an audience, even if a rude heckler provokes you. An attack on any single member of the audience is perceived as an attack upon all. If you stay calm and let the heckler attack you, the audience will move to your side. Be patient because the heckler is counting on you losing control in some way. Be 'Zen-like' and let them have their time; acknowledge their point of view, and then move on.

Don't ever call upon an associate or a colleague in the audience to answer a question you can't handle, unless he or she has given you prior permission to do so, and has agreed to be available for assistance. The potential embarrassment of a colleague could cause the audience to distrust you, and certainly your colleague will.

Don't forget that you're talking to real, live human beings, just like yourself. They don't expect you to be perfect any more than you expect perfection of other speakers. What most business people are looking for is honest, easy-to-understand conversation, delivered clearly and concisely. Don't try to be someone else. The audience is looking for authentic self-expression.

Rehearsal and Practice

> *The world is your exercise book.*
> —Richard Bach, *Illusions*

Probably the best way to prepare yourself for delivering a presentation is with a tape recorder. First, go over your talk without an audience, just speaking in a normal conversational voice into the tape. You'll learn a lot from your first playback. Listen as if you were in the audience, and don't be too critical. You are likely to be far more critical of yourself than most audiences would be.

On your second run through, once you've got used to hearing your own voice, concentrate on staying close to your time limit and making smooth transitions from one point to the next.

On your third taping, have at least one person in the room. Do it standing up and speak loudly and clearly, just as you will in the actual situation. Recording your practice sessions is one of the most powerful things you can do. It gives you instant feedback and understanding of how you sound, and gets you used to your own voice. However, nothing can take the place of someone listening and actually giving you immediate feedback. Choose the feedback person carefully, selecting someone you trust who has a similar style to yours. If this is a critical event, hire a professional.

You are likely to discover content changes you wish to make as you go over your talk in a practice phase. Make a fresh set of notes, then have your script entirely re-typed to reflect your final version. This is the one you deliver. Make clean, clear and easy-to-read notes. These are important when you're facing an audience.

Be sure to complete your final practice session before the day of your presentation. You'll get very little benefit from last-minute practice. If possible, use the few hours before you speak to reflect on the concepts and major theme of your presentation and to visualize yourself giving your presentation successfully, with power and enthusiasm. See yourself doing it, in the same way that Olympic athletes visualize themselves winning.

It's a good idea to visit the physical location of your presentation a day ahead—or earlier. Your subconscious will adjust to the exact dimensions and dynamics of the room in which you're going to give your speech, letting the environment sink in and reinforcing your visualization.

To prepare for possible tough questions, have someone play the role of devil's advocate. Have a friend or an associate prepare a list of questions based on your talk. Then have someone read these questions to you. The key to this practice technique is listening to the questions that have been phrased by someone else. This isn't exactly what you'll face in the real situation, however it will prepare you well.

Avoid videotaping yourself since many people are more critical of what they see than what they hear. What they tend to notice is the distracting body language, gestures, uncomfortable and inhibited mannerisms and facial expressions. The first question they usually ask me is, "What do I do with my hands?" The answer is: use your hands to make natural gestures just as you do in a normal conversation, only make them slightly broader or bigger. Small gestures appear tentative and uncertain when you're in front of a group.

I have seen serious damage done to the individual in videotape feedback sessions, as a result of trying to force the person to sound or look the same as the instructor or the most experienced presenter in the company. We can only become effective by being ourselves, and should never try to become presentation clones. The audience knows the difference between phoniness and authenticity.

When you're not using your hands to make relevant gestures or to lead the audience's attention towards visuals, keep them loosely by your sides. If you have good rapport with your audience, you can put your hands in your pockets, however this does restrict your movements. (If you do put your hands in your pockets, make sure you've taken out any coins or other objects which might rattle and distract your audience.) Above all else, be natural, just as if you are having a conversation with friends.

Avoid the 'fig leaf' stance, standing with your hands clasped in front of you. It tends to look defensive and gives the impression that you're apprehensive and lack conviction. And avoid the reverse 'fig leaf'—hands clasped behind you, unless you are doing an imitation of Prince Phillip (this stance has become his trademark). This tends to look professorial and gives the impression that you're lecturing the audience. The audience does not like to be lectured; they want to be informed, but not told what to do.

One gesture to avoid is pointing a finger directly at a member of the audience. This feels intimidating and, to some people, quite threatening. Even though you're only singling someone out for a friendly purpose, the effect of this particular gesture is nearly always negative. Using the open palm, and pointing all of your fingers, or your hand in general, towards the individual appears much more friendly and welcoming.

The strongest impression a speaker can make on an audience is usually at the visual level. A gesture, whether intended or not, is apt to have as great an effect on listeners as the words you are speaking. So either make relevant, productive gestures, or relax and make none at all.

Speaking to Young People

> *What comes from the heart touches the heart.*
> —Don Sibet

Business presenters are occasionally asked to speak to a young audience, ranging from campers, to youth associations, and school groups of all ages. Never turn down the opportunity to speak to groups like these. Such occasions are often the most potent learning experiences for public speakers. This is because children detect and reject insincerity instantly. This is true of all ages, from toddlers right through to teenagers. Speaking to young listeners will help you communicate naturally and directly. It will help you to become a more authentic speaker.

Bear in mind the following points when addressing a young audience.

- **Avoid being superior.** Don't talk down to young people. Condescension is another form of phoniness and kids don't like it. If you want to get a message across, be real; they know the difference.

- **Be on their level.** The younger the audience, the more important it is to connect with them at eye level. If you're trying to communicate with a four- or five-year-old, sit down on a chair or even on the floor. With children, there's virtually no communication without direct eye contact or visual reinforcement.

- **Use straight talk.** Confucius said, "The ultimate evil is the ability to make abstract that which is concrete." In other words, with regard to children, straight talk about real things and real objects is what's required. They like people with names and faces. They get impatient with generalizations.

- **Involve them.** If you want to communicate effectively with teenagers, get them involved during your talk, with a free-wheeling conversation, Socratic in style. Teenagers have great energy and imagination. Go for direction rather than control when speaking to a roomful of teenagers. It is an adult illusion that you can control what they think. They are smarter and more informed than any generation preceding them, so treat them with respect, and they will treat you accordingly.

- **Remember when…** Because there's still a child in each of us, the lessons we learn from speaking to young listeners are directly applicable to our communication with an adult audience, even in a business environment. Be open, honest and sincere. Keep your eyes on your listeners' eyes. Avoid abstractions. Get your listeners involved in what you are talking about. Authentic self-expression is admired and respected, so stand up and speak out.

What Audiences Appreciate

When you have been asked to speak on a subject that you are an expert on, make your opening remarks relevant to your point of view, not to the audience or the city where you're speaking. That may be appropriate later in the middle of your talk, however you've been asked to speak because you're an expert on a specific topic, so start on a businesslike note.

Pause before you open your mouth to speak, and focus your eyes on one person in the audience, preferably someone about halfway to the back or in the first ten rows. The pause will get their attention and direct your attention to someone in the middle of the room. You will automatically speak louder than if you had fixed on somebody in the front row.

You have about three-to-five minutes to convince the audience that you've got something interesting to say. Find an interesting opening statement or a compelling first sentence. One of the sources that you can use is *Peter's Book of Quotations* by Lawrence Peter.

Don't risk losing the effect of your planned opening statement by trying to respond to the remarks of the previous speaker. Stay on track. It's safer to stick to your rehearsed and familiar opening, no matter how tempting it might be to change it.

The Use of Humor

> *It costs nothing, but creates much. It enriches those who receive it without impoverishing those who give. It happens in a flash, and the memory of it sometimes lasts forever. Yet it cannot be bought, borrowed or stolen, for it is something that is no earthly good to anyone until it is given away. And if, in the course of the day, some of your friends should be too tired to give you a smile, why don't you give them one of yours? For nobody needs a smile as much as those who have none left to give.*
> *Smile.*
>
> —Anonymous

Humor is one of the most difficult tools to use in a presentation. Using it effectively requires timing and lots of rehearsal.

I remember watching Bob Hope on the *Johnny Carson Show* practicing a joke in front of Carson, and saying, "What did you think?" Carson replied, "Well it's not quite right." Hope then revealed that he'd been practicing the timing on that joke and still didn't have it right. Being a stand-up comedian is an art mastered by only a few lifetime professionals, and if you're not one of them, why risk making a fool of yourself in the attempt?

The safest approach for the average business presenter is to avoid attempts at humor as they are likely doomed to fail and therefore make the audience nervous.

If you do choose to use humor in your presentation, here are some helpful guidelines:

- Your humor should always be appropriate and relevant to your point of view.
- Always balance your professionalism with your humanness.
- Use your own personal stories, observations or humorous asides for a light-hearted approach.
- Laugh at yourself and enjoy it with the audience.
- Humor should only be directed at yourself.
- Be aware of any slang or colloquialism that might be offensive.
- Never use a member of the audience as the butt of a joke.

The most natural expression of humor is the simple smile. And since most smiles are started by other smiles, make a point of smiling at least a couple of times during your talk, especially at the beginning. By relaxing, you'll naturally be more humorous. Don't worry about deliberately incorporating humor. Most speakers find something naturally funny to laugh at during a talk, like an upside-down slide or a Freudian slip, or even forgetting your own name, or something humorous that members of the audience throw in, intentionally or not, during a Q&A period. Most importantly, don't take yourself too seriously, and your natural sense of humor will come through when you're relaxed and engaging in your presentation.

Introducing Another Speaker

You are here for a purpose.
There is no duplicate of you in the whole wide world.
There never has been.
There never will be.
You were brought here now to fulfill a certain need.
Take time to think that one over.
— Lou Austin

Unless it is a formal occasion, you don't have to thank the person introducing you or thank the audience for coming. That often seems insincere. It will be a pleasant surprise for your listeners if you jump right in to your powerful opening sentence, and will automatically identify you as a no-nonsense, competent presenter.

The key to an effective introduction is to give the audience a reason to listen. Let them know why the speaker you are introducing is someone of interest. This information usually has nothing to do with where he or she went to school or how many kids they've got, etc.

Tell them that they're about to hear from an expert and then relay the information that makes that person an expert, i.e. their qualifications, and how much experience they've had.

Make sure you obtain these details from the speaker before you start.

In the case of testimonial or award introductions, when the recipient is going to give an acceptance speech, the introduction is a mini-speech itself. Your best plan is to get a detailed résumé from the speaker. If you don't know the person, interview him or her by phone to get some additional interesting material. Better still, interview one or two acquaintances of the person and build a personal profile; when you're giving an introduction to a testimonial, it's usually a testimonial to the character and qualities of the person you are introducing.

Don't say, "Our guest speaker needs no introduction." This is incorrect. You're there to do the introduction! This is presumptuous and rude to the audience.

Be different. Come right out with the speaker's name. "Mary Smith is not only a key executive of _____, she is a leading authority on _____." Everybody already knows his/her name (usually there's a printed program), so why pretend you're building to a surprise by waiting until the end of the introduction to give the speaker's name?

Double-check information in résumés and newspaper clippings. Facts change: people get divorced or widowed, and change job titles, affiliations, and political parties. Everyone gains new resources, and creates new headlines.

If you're introducing a colleague who's well known to most of the attendees, such as a fellow-executive in the same company, use the opportunity to say something new about him or her. Part of your job is to get the speaker off to a good start and even old friends appreciate thoughtful introductions.

'911' Emergency Tactics

> *Fear: the best way out is through.*
> —Helen Keller

When I was starting out as a speaker, I would sometimes find myself at a loss, tongue-tied or completely blank, either from fatigue or poor preparation. An old pro gave me some life-saving strategies, and I share them for that rare occasion when you need '911'.

Use only in emergencies, and use them sparingly, otherwise the audience will know you are stalling. The following stalling techniques will help you gain thinking time or regain control of the presentation if you get confused or off track:

- Remove your glasses, then proceed to clean them.
- Scratch your head as if deep in thought.
- Ask loudly, "Can you hear me at the back?"
- State, "Let me rephrase that," or "Let me put it this way."
- Use any of the following: "The correct title is...", "I will repeat that..." or "It seems to me that...", "I am going to modify that statement to make my point," "Let me explain that...," "As I was saying...," "What I am saying is...".

The best laid plans can come apart sometimes. Don't worry about it; re-focus on your long-term goals and vision. Most audiences have experienced moments of confusion or distraction in similar situations, so keep going and keep caring. If *you* do, *they* will.

Have fun and get great results.

Epilogue

Our deepest fear is not that we are inadequate.
Our deepest fear is that we are powerful
beyond measure.
It is our light, not our darkness,
that frightens us.
We ask ourselves, "who am I to be brilliant,
gorgeous, talented, and fabulous?"
Actually, who are you not to be?
You are a child of God.
Your playing small doesn't serve the world.
There is nothing enlightened about shrinking so
that other people won't feel insecure around you.
We are all meant to shine, as children do.
We were born to manifest the glory of God
that is within us.
It's not just in some of us; it's in everyone.
And as we let our own light shine,
we unconsciously give other people permission
to do the same.
As we are liberated from our own fear,
our presence automatically liberates others.

—Marianne Williamson
from *A Return to Love*

Bibliography

A Manual for Life
Bennet Wong & Jock
McKeen
PD Seminars.

*The Seven Habits of
Highly Effective People*
Stephen R. Covey
Simon & Schuster

Boom, Bust & Echo
David K. Foot
Macfarlane, Walter & Ross

*The Fifth Discipline
Fieldbook*
Peter Senge
Currency Doubleday

New Passages
Gail Sheehy
Random House of Canada

The New Positioning
Jack Trout
McGraw-Hill

The One-to-One Future
Peppers and Rogers
Currency Doubleday

*Perfectionism: what's bad
about being too good?*
M. Adderholdt-Elliott, PhD
Free Spirit Publishing

Sex in the Snow
M. Adams
Penguin

Shakedown
Angus Reid
Seal Books

Timeless Healing
Herbert Benson, MD
Scribner

*You Can Do It:
how to encourage yourself*
Lewis E. Losconcy
Prentice Hall Press

Communicating in person is the most powerful form of human interaction. Those with the ability, skill and courage to effectively present their ideas and information have a distinct edge. They can motivate, persuade and make things happen!

About the Author, Geoffrey Lane

Geoffrey Lane is a passionate advocate of the power of authentic self-expression. His career as a professional speaker and trainer began with his early experience as a spokesperson for an international cosmetics firm. Speaking at trade shows, Geoffrey developed his presentation skills the hard way—addressing audiences comprised of his customers and competitors.

As his reputation as a speaker grew, Geoffrey became more involved in coaching and training others in the art of making effective presentations. His ability to connect with his audience took him to Context Associated where he facilitated personal and professional self-development seminars for five years. The inspiration for creating a new and unique approach to developing presentation skills came from Geoffrey's work as a successful speaker and dedicated coach. Based on more than 27 years of experience and research, the NuSpeak program offers practical strategies and techniques that work.

Geoffrey Lane is the founder and president of NuMethod Education Inc. In addition to leading seminars and writing about modern presentation skills, he is a frequent guest speaker and resident lecturer at the University of British Columbia.

About the NuSpeak Philosophy

NuSpeak is grounded in the principles of authenticity and personal commitment as the keys to effective communication. The program is dedicated to improving self-awareness and developing the use of presentation skills and abilities on as broad a base as possible, towards the goal of creating a more committed and caring community.

"By working together, you developed for me a noticeable improvement in my presentations to a number of different audiences over a broad range of issues. Based on audience feedback, the results have demonstrated a measurable improvement."

Donald A. Calder, President & CEO, BCTel

Show Up and Be Heard . . . at a NuSpeak Workshop!

Now that you've read about the NuSpeak approach, experience the difference by participating in a workshop. You'll discover that great presentations are not just a matter of talent—there are practical tools and techniques that can help you master your fears and speak with confidence.

NuSpeak is based on the experiential learning model and is grounded in the principles of authenticity and personal commitment. The program is designed to create a positive, supportive environment that encourages change and reinforces each speaker's authentic presentation style.

Learn skills for engaging, persuading and inspiring your audience.

At the NuSpeak workshop, you will learn realistic strategies and techniques that will help you overcome the psychological blocks you face when speaking to groups. And by practicing these strategies during the workshop session, you'll gain the confidence and power to become a more dynamic communicator.

We believe so strongly in the power of the NuSpeak experience that we invite participants to repeat the workshop in six months, free of charge.

To get information on NuSpeak workshop dates and locations, visit our website, at www.numethod.com, or fax us your request.

"Despite having over 30 years of public speaking experience, I received substantial new information and I found the program to be very rewarding and fun. Regardless of the participants' speaking experience, we all benefited immensely. For myself, I especially found value in being provided with a track to run on so that I could always pick up the thread of my message despite any asides and interruptions."

Patrick Hunt, Maximizer Software

"The format of your workshop, complemented by your excellent examples and direction, as well as the small class size, all made for a very powerful experience. I highly recommend your workshop to others, at all levels of experience."

W. D. Johnson, CGA, FCIS, P. Admin., Director of Education & Student Services,
Certified General Accountants Association of British Columbia

"I personally came away with the feeling of "Yes, I can do it!""

Franziska Kaltenegger, President, International Conference Services Ltd.

To order additional books or to receive information on the NuSpeak Workshop

❏ Please send me additional copies of
NuSpeak—Become a Powerful Speaker

❏ **Yes!** I want to become a more powerful speaker. Please send
me more information about the next NuSpeak Workshop

Name _____

Title_____ Company_____

Address _____

City _____ State _____ Zip_____

Telephone ( ) _____

Fax ( ) _____ E-mail_____

Please send me____ copies of **NuSpeak—Become a Powerful Speaker**

I enclose:

US $19.95 per book _____

Applicable sales tax _____

Base shipping cost US $3.00

Plus US $0.95 per book for handling _____

Total _____

Payment Method ❏ VISA   Card #_____

❏ MasterCard   Expiration date_____

❏ American Express

Signature_____